Blood Brothers

Methuen Drama publications for GCSE students

Available and forthcoming

GCSE Student Editions

Willy Russell's *Blood Brothers*
Simon Stephens's *The Curious Incident of the Dog in the Night-Time*
Charlotte Keatley's *My Mother Said I Never Should*
Shelagh Delaney's *A Taste of Honey*

GCSE Student Guides

Willy Russell's *Blood Brothers* by Ros Merkin
Simon Stephens's *The Curious Incident of the Dog in the Night-Time* by Jacqueline Bolton
Dennis Kelly's *DNA* by Maggie Inchley
Alan Bennett's *The History Boys* by Steve Nicholson
J. B. Priestley's *An Inspector Calls* by Philip Roberts
R. C. Sherriff's *Journey's End* by Andrew Maunder
Charlotte Keatley's *My Mother Said I Never Should* by Sophie Bush
Shelagh Delaney's *A Taste of Honey* by Kate Whittaker

Blood Brothers GCSE Student Guide

ROS MERKIN

Series Editor: Jenny Stevens

Bloomsbury Methuen Drama
An imprint of Bloomsbury Publishing Plc

B L O O M S B U R Y
LONDON · OXFORD · NEW YORK · NEW DELHI · SYDNEY

Bloomsbury Methuen Drama

An imprint of Bloomsbury Publishing Plc
Imprint previously known as Methuen Drama

50 Bedford Square 1385 Broadway
London New York
WC1B 3DP NY 10018
UK USA

www.bloomsbury.com

**BLOOMSBURY, METHUEN DRAMA and the Diana logo are
trademarks of Bloomsbury Publishing Plc**

British Library Cataloguing-in-Publication Data
A catalogue record for this book is available from the British Library.

ISBN: PB: 978-1-4742-2998-2
ePDF: 978-1-4742-3001-8
epub: 978-1-4742-30025

Library of Congress Cataloging-in-Publication Data
A catalog record for this book is available from the Library of Congress

Typeset by RefineCatch Limited, Bungay, Suffolk

CONTENTS

CHAPTER ONE

The Play

Introduction: Reading drama

Reading a play is a strange thing to do mostly because a play text (the book you hold in your hands), unlike a novel, is not a finished thing. Instead it functions as a blueprint for a performance, a set of instructions for directors and actors and designers to create a performance for an audience to watch and listen to. When you are reading a play you are being asked to use your imagination, to see how a character might look and sound and move, to picture the places and spaces they might inhabit on a stage. The writer does, of course, give you lots and lots of clues and your job in reading is to try and work out how these might all work in practice and also to think about what is happening in-between the lines. Don't forget that if you are in a theatre watching a play, even when they are not speaking, the actors playing the characters are still visible to an audience. Something is still happening.

The information comes in two ways. There is the *dialogue* or what characters say to each other. There are also the *stage directions*. These might give you information on how the lines are to be spoken or what a character is doing or where a scene is set. The temptation when reading is to skip over these bits (which in a script are usually in italics) to concentrate on and prioritize what the characters are saying. This means you would miss important moments in the play. For example, in

Blood Brothers, you would miss the moment where Mrs Johnstone agrees to allow Mrs Lyons to have one of the twins. She never says yes. She simply '*nods*' (38). Or, later, you would miss Mickey battling to stop taking his tablets, as during the song 'Light Romance', the stage directions tell us

> *Throughout the following chorus we see* MICKEY *at work. We see him go to take his pills. We see him make the effort of not taking them. We see the strain of this upon him but see that he is determined.* (130–131)

So, the stage directions are important both in terms of plot (what happens) but also in terms of character and you cannot afford to miss either.

If you bear in mind when you are reading that while a book *tells* us a story, a piece of theatre (which is what a play text is destined to be) *shows* us a story or re-presents it in front of us, this will help remind you to think about what you might be hearing and seeing. After all, the two words we use for people who go to the theatre (audience and spectator) come from words that mean to listen and to watch. The best way to really understand a play is to act it out. It might not be possible in your school, although even the tiniest space will be enough to try things out. If you cannot act the play out, then you might have to make do with reading it aloud, in which case it is useful to have someone reading the stage directions and to discuss what sort of space each scene is happening in.

Overview

Things to do

- Think about the title of the play and make a list of all the expectations you have about the play from the title.

Russell presents us with two problems that can make reading the play difficult. Firstly, the play is divided into two acts but whilst there are clearly different scenes, these are not marked in the script as they are in many plays. He has obviously written like this for a reason; it makes the narrative a seamless, inevitable whole that moves relentlessly to the conclusion, but it can make it hard to follow. When she is directing, Glen Walford breaks the play into eighty-two units (or sections). Whilst that number of sections might make things just as confusing, it is useful to think about how you might break the play down into parts to help you study the text. What follows uses the ages of the twins as an organizing device. Secondly, he provides no specific dates. There are some clues in the text, for example, the mention of pounds, shillings and pence (decimalization happened in 1971) and he has said that when the narrator talks about today near the end of the play, that relates to the time of the play's first production. Whilst it is hard to be very specific about dates, it is possible to identify which decade each section takes place in.

Prologue (pp. 29–30)

Time: 1950s (including a moment in the 1980s)

The play starts at the end, the outline of two bodies marked out on the stage. This means the audience know how it all ends before it has even started, suggesting a fatalism (it will be like this and nothing can change it) and allowing them to concentrate on HOW and WHY it happens rather than WHAT happens. Mrs Johnstone is introduced. She looks old but in the past she danced and was lovelier (and sexier) than Marilyn Monroe. Then her husband walked out on her to dance with someone else, leaving seven children and one more on the way. A sympathy is set up with her plight and two key motifs (dancing and Marilyn Monroe) are introduced.

Section 1: The twins are born and parted (pp. 30–48)

Time: Late 1950s/early 1960s

Mrs Johnstone cannot even dream of happiness without real life getting in the way and the milkman demanding payment interrupts her reminiscences. She has not got enough money to pay him. From offstage, the children complain and alone onstage Mrs Johnstone tries to appease them. However, there is a promise that things will get better. She has a new job and will be able to feed them. Arriving for her first day at work, the play juxtaposes Mrs Lyons and Mrs Johnstone putting the two characters next to each other to emphasize the differences between them; Mrs Lyons has new shoes but cannot have children and Mrs Johnstone has a duster and a brush and cannot stop having children. It also introduces the theme of superstition as Mrs Lyons puts her new shoes on the table, the moment underlined by the narrator.

Shocked to find out she is having twins, Mrs Johnstone's hopes that she was getting straight are dashed but Mrs Lyons forms a plan to help them both. She offers to take one of the babies, and, before Mrs Johnstone has even agreed, is stuffing a cushion under her dress to simulate a pregnancy and planning what to tell her husband. Mrs Johnstone nods her agreement as she realizes that the child will have everything. She can see Mrs Lyons is desperate and is promised she will be able to see the child every day when she comes to work. Mrs Lyons insists that it must be a binding agreement and makes Mrs Johnstone swear on the Bible. Once again, the narrator adds to the tension and for the first time we hear a phrase that will recur: 'a debt is a debt and must be paid' (40). The optimism at the start has evaporated and with the birth of the babies there is little to celebrate.

Arriving back home from the hospital with the twins, Mrs Johnstone is met by the debt collectors. She is behind with her payments and the dawning realization through the song 'Easy Terms' is it is not just her furniture that is going to be repossessed. Mrs Lyons arrives to collect her baby. Mrs Johnstone tries to buy some time because 'they're a pair, they go together', but Mrs Lyons is insistent (42). Not wanting to know which baby she takes, Mrs Johnstone agrees. Going home with Mickey, the remaining twin, she explains to her other children that the other twin has gone to heaven, one of many lies that are woven through the text.

Mrs Johnstone goes back to work but Mrs Lyons is agitated, her fear of Mrs Johnstone clear. She tells her husband that she wants to fire the cleaner because she is acting like the baby's mother. Mr Lyons is concerned she is depressed, an intimation about her later mental state. Getting money from her husband, she sacks Mrs Johnstone, trying to pay her off. A desperate Mrs Johnstone faced with losing her job and no longer being able to see her son, threatens to take her child back or to tell someone. Increasingly fearful, Mrs Lyons tries to stop her and when all else fails, knowing that Mrs Johnstone is superstitious, concocts a story that sounds like an old tale: if the children learn they were once a pair, both will immediately die. It is another lie. The narrator underlines the ominous undertones, warning that 'the devil's got your number' (47). A fearful Mrs Johnstone returns home and locks herself in.

Section 2: Aged seven (but nearly eight) (pp. 48–81)

Time: Seven years later. The mid- to late 1960s

Mickey is banished to play by the front door, his mother angry he has been playing near the big houses in the park, where she knows Edward lives. He is bored and lonely, wishing he was his older brother Sammy. His boredom is broken by Edward who has seen him playing near the park. Mickey demands sweets which Edward readily gives and quickly, through

Edward's delight at Mickey's swearing and stories, a bond forms. When they discover they were born on the same day, they swear to be blood brothers. They are interrupted by Sammy brandishing a toy gun and then discovered by Mrs Johnstone who, on realizing who Edward is, tells him to beat it or the bogey man will get him.

Back home, Edward reaches for his dictionary to look up the new word. His mother insists there is no such thing as a bogey man. At this moment, Mickey appears wanting to play. Mrs Lyons works out who Mickey is and when Edward declares he likes Mickey more than her, Mrs Lyons hits him 'instinctively' (60). Edward remains alone, watching, while the children play games on the street with guns, foreshadowing later events. Part of the gang is Linda, who stands up to Sammy and then defends and comforts Mickey when all the others turn on him.

Left alone with Linda, Mickey produces the airgun he has stolen from Sammy and they go in search of Edward, persuading him, despite his mother's forbidding, to go to the park. The gang is forming and Edward is excited by their bravado.

The narrator sets the mood for the following scene suggesting '[t]hey're gonna take your baby away' (67). Mrs Lyons, distraught to discover Edward missing, calls her husband home from work. He thinks she is over protective and should get something for her nerves. She is convinced that Edward is 'drawn' to 'these people' but she cannot explain the truth to him (69). Instead, she tells him she is frightened and wants to move. As they talk, he puts a pair of shoes on the table. She sweeps them off, seemingly affected by Mrs Johnstone's superstitious beliefs, an idea underlined by the narrator. The devil is still going to find them.

Unaware of this, the children are playing. Mickey stops them firing the gun because Linda seems to be the only one who can hit the target and they move on to throwing stones through windows but get caught by a policeman. Edward, not realizing the other two have been boasting earlier, says his name is Adolf

Hitler. They are all taken home in tears by the policeman, who then deals very differently with the two families.

Persuaded by the encounter with the policeman that they should move, Mr Lyons breaks the news to Edward claiming it is because 'Mummy's not been too well' (72). Edward, going to say goodbye to Mickey, is met by Mrs Johnstone. She tries to encourage him, saying he will love his new house and make new friends. Edward says he will never forget them. She gives him a locket with a picture of Mickey and herself, making him promise to keep it a secret. He confesses he used to think 'you weren't very nice' but now he thinks she is 'smashin'', showing the growing bond between mother and son (75). As Edward says goodbye to Mickey, giving him the toy gun his father bought him, he sets off unenthusiastically to the country.

Left in the city, Mickey misses his friend. In his garden in the country, Edward is equally bored and alone. Their duet shows their connections and an appreciation of their differences. The dejection is broken by good news. Mrs Johnstone is being rehoused to the country and 'Bright New Day' suggests a return to the optimism of the start of the show for the Johnstone family. The Act ends on this joyful, positive note, with Mrs Johnstone convinced that they are starting all over again. The narrator's warnings about the devil seem not to have been borne out.

Section 3: The teenage years: being fourteen (pp. 82–104)

Time: Late 1960s to early 1970s

The start of Act Two is still optimistic. Mrs Johnstone is dancing again and teasing Mickey who is an awkward fourteen-year-old, self-conscious about his appearance. She has not forgotten her other son although she has not seen him for years. The joyous Johnstone house stands in contrast to the Lyons' where a rather stiff and still fearful Mrs Lyons is teaching Edward to waltz before he goes back to boarding school. At the Johnstone's, the concern is to get Mickey to school and to Linda who is waiting for him at the bus stop. Their relationship is developing, and after Sammy is chased off by the police for pulling a knife on the bus conductor, Linda tells Mickey she loves him and does not care who knows, much to Mickey's embarrassment.

The following two scenes show the differences between the schools the twins attend and, at the same time, the similarities between the boys. Edward has a promising future but is suspended for refusing to take off his locket. Mickey is suspended for saying school is boring and questioning the usefulness of the education he is getting. Receiving the letter about Edward's suspension, Mrs Lyons discovers that the locket contains pictures of Mickey and Mrs Johnstone but Edward will not tell her where he got it from. It is, he tells her, a secret, and everybody's got secrets. The audience, in on the truth, will see the irony here. The tension is once again raised by the narrator. The devil is getting closer.

Mickey and Linda go for a walk. She tries to get him to return her feelings. He is too self-conscious so she tries to make him jealous, before abandoning him. Mickey wishes he was more like the boy he can see in the window and the boy wishes he was more like Mickey before they recognize each other. The twins are reunited. Edward offers to help Mickey find the words to say to Linda, suggesting they go and see 'how it's done' at the films (97). They go off happily to get some money from Mickey's house but Mrs Lyons has seen them and follows them, with the narrator reminding her that there are debts to be paid. At Mrs Johnstone's, the boys try to cover up what film they are going to see, in a scene that suggests a warmth and closeness between the three of them. As they leave, Mrs Lyons breaks Mrs Johnstone's good mood, confronting her and accusing her of following them. Her neurosis and her sadness at having a son who will never really be hers bursts to the surface and when Mrs Johnstone refuses to be paid off again she lunges at her with a kitchen knife, cursing her as a witch, in one of the major confrontations of the play.

Leaving the cinema dazzled by what they have seen, the twins bump into Linda and her friend. There is a moment of good humour which culminates in them all cheeking the policeman. Now, the gang of three is reunited. Things look optimistic again.

Interlude: Summer sun: the teenage years (pp. 104–110)

Time: Early to mid-1970s

In a sequence led by the narrator, the happiest part of the play unfolds over a series of summers which take the twins from fourteen to eighteen. There is lots of fun (a funfair, sharing dreams and taking funny photographs). There are also hints of what is to come as Linda finds herself caught in the middle of the boys in a game of piggy-in-the-middle and Edward finally, if cautiously, tells her that he loves her although he knows that she loves Mickey. However, the narrator is ready to remind the audience of the tragedy to come. If the teenagers cannot see the broken bottle in the sand, the audience must not forget that they are there. The sequence ends in an upbeat mood. Edward, about to leave for university, finally gets Mickey to ask Linda out and heads off with promises of Christmas parties to come.

Section 4: Adults (pp. 110–130)

Time: Late 1970s to early 1980s

Everything is quickly brought back down to reality and the pace of the story picks up as it moves towards the conclusion that we have known was inevitable. Linda is pregnant. She and Mickey marry, the wedding colliding with Mickey being made redundant. It is just a sign of the times, as the stage fills with others on the dole. Christmas approaches. Edward returns from university ready for the parties but is met by a very different Mickey with nothing to celebrate. Explaining the realities of life on the dole to Edward, the scene shows the growing gap between the two. They argue for the first time. Mickey faced with the harsh realities of adult life sees Edward as still being a child and pushes him away. Bumping in to Linda as he leaves, Edward also discovers that they are married. This encounter is intercut with Sammy persuading Mickey to be a lookout for him and as the pace picks up even more (and the narrator reminds the audience that there is no getting off without the price being paid), the scene explodes into the shooting of a man and Mickey and Sammy being arrested.

In prison, Mickey becomes depressed and the parallels with Marilyn Monroe's life are returned to, although this time not suggesting the earlier happiness. Addicted to anti-depressants, Mickey gets out of prison but just as he has pushed Edward away, so he pushes Linda away. She tries to help him by getting him a job and a house from someone she knows. Although she does not admit who this is, the audience (and Mickey) know Edward is handing out things again, just as earlier he handed out sweets. Pushed even further by Mickey's refusal to stop taking the drugs and worn down by life, Linda is drawn to Edward and they start a light romance.

Mrs Lyons sees what is happening and shows Mickey and from this moment the stage explodes in panic. In his hunt for Edward, Mickey breaks '*through groups of people, looking, searching*' (126). Mrs Johnstone is screaming and banging on Linda's door shouting for her. The narrator is telling us that a man has gone mad and the devil's 'callin' your number up today/Today/Today/TODAY!' (126–7). They are moving relentlessly towards their fate. The final confrontation starts more calmly. Mickey, armed with Sammy's gun, interrupts Edward at the council. He can see clearly now he has stopped taking the pills and is convinced Edward, who has got everything while he has nothing, is trying to take away Linda, the last thing he has left. Any talk of their friendship is now in the past tense. For a brief moment, things look as though they might not end up as we expect. Mickey admits he cannot even shoot Edward, nor does he know if the gun is loaded. It is the arrival of Mrs Johnstone that final brings everything falling down. When she tells them the truth, Mickey realizes he too could have had everything and with a despairing howl of rage he waves his gun at Edward, blowing him apart. Mickey is killed by four guns fired by the police. Mrs Johnstone is left to survey her two dead sons wishing it had all been a scene 'from an old movie of Marilyn Monroe' (130).

Things to do

- In small groups try to tell the story of the play taking turns to add a sentence. This could also be done as a written exercise where you allow yourself a limited number of sentences to tell the story.

- Make a list of the ten most important moments in the play in the order they happen. In class, you can try to create still images of these moments and show them to the rest of the class. See which other moments different groups might have picked and create a 'final' list in the class which everyone agrees with.

- Write the 'blurb' for the back of a new edition of *Blood Brothers*, thinking about what might encourage someone to want to read the play.

Context

Production history

- November 1981: Original version, with one song, performed at schools around Merseyside by Merseyside Young People's Theatre.

- 8 January 1983: Rewritten version with songs opened at Liverpool Playhouse, running for twelve weeks.

- 11 April 1983: Transferred to the Lyric Theatre in London's West End running until 22 October 1983.

- 28 July 1988: Following two national tours, reopened at the Albery Theatre, London, produced by Bill Kenwright, transferring to the Phoenix Theatre in 1991 running for twenty-four years, closing on 27 October 2012.

- International productions have included America, Australia, Japan, South Korea, Russia, Poland, Israel, Germany, Holland and Denmark. In 2014, it was adapted by David Kramer for performances in South Africa, the first time that Willy Russell had allowed the musical to be adapted.

Political context

1. Thatcher

In 1979, Margaret Thatcher arrived at 10 Downing Street, the first woman prime minister in British history. She became one of the few prime ministers to have a political system named after them and Thatcherism set out to right the problems of the country through deregulation (removing government controls), cuts in spending and taxes and privatization (selling off assets). One of Thatcher's central political beliefs was a determination to make people stand on their own two feet, to look after themselves rather than to be dependent on the state and on welfare. This was combined with a belief that success came to those who chose to work hard. The focus was on the individual, an idea summed up in an interview for *Woman's Own* in 1987 when she declared 'there's no such thing as society [. . .] only individual men and women and their families'. People, she continued, must look after themselves first.

One impact of Thatcherism was unemployment which rose to three million in January 1983 (one-in-eight of the work-force), a figure which it did not go below until 1987. Hardest hit was Northern Ireland, closely followed by northern England and Scotland. It was a political system that split the country (she is sometimes called the Marmite Prime Minister). Some people did make lots of money, particularly in the City of London. Others felt as though they benefitted from Thatcher through schemes such as the Right to Buy which allowed council house tenants to buy their houses for anything up to a 70 per cent discount. Others resisted her policies and one defining event of the Thatcher era was the 1984–5 Miners Strike. It was 'one of the most bloody and tragic disputes of modern times', in which Thatcher took on and beat the union with the closure of 150 pits and the decimation of the communities associated with them (Marr, 2008, 411).

2. The 1970s

It is possible to characterize *Blood Brothers* as a critique of Thatcherism but whilst this reflects when the play was first produced, in the play, Mickey is faced with losing his job in an earlier decade, the 1970s, when the Labour Party was in power. Labour had formed the government in 1974 with a very small majority at a time when the economy was in trouble and inflation was high (24 per cent in 1975). They faced a series of financial crisis and were forced to borrow money, a loan which came with strings attached including cuts in public spending (i.e. welfare and education). Unemployment started to rise although it was never as bad as it later became under the Tories (it averaged 4 per cent during the decade) but manufacturing industry was in decline and many familiar household names disappeared. The 1970s ended in The Winter of Discontent when public sector workers struck, refusing an imposed pay rise. There are two abiding images of this winter: rubbish piling up on the streets and the dead not being buried. The latter occurred in Liverpool where over 300 bodies were piled up in cold storage as the council discussed emergency plans to dispose of them at sea or even to ask relatives to dig their own graves. The result of all this upheaval was the election which Thatcher won, during which the Tories used a poster which has become one of the most famous election posters. It shows a snaking dole queue above which is the slogan 'Labour Isn't Working'.

3. Liverpool

Russell has always been at pains to argue that *Blood Brothers* is not just a Liverpool play and its international success is a testament to its universality. He maintains,

> I just happen to write in Liverpool but I use Liverpool as a metaphor for wherever. I know it's the same in Bradford, I know it's the same in Burnley, I know it's the same in Glasgow and Newcastle. All right they have geographical, regional, idiomatic differences, but the stories I tell set in Liverpool are stories that happen in other languages in Bradford, Burnley, Glasgow and Newcastle.

> GILL, 1992, 1

But, the play is set in Liverpool and was first performed in Liverpool so whilst the more general context is relevant, it is also important to look at how it specifically impacted on Liverpool. The negative effects of Thatcherism were particularly felt in the north of the country (note the cities Russell chooses to mention above) which were the manufacturing heartland of the country. The unemployment of the 1970s and 1980s hit Liverpool particularly hard. Dependent for jobs on the docks and manufacturing industry, much trade moved from America to Europe and Liverpool's docks, being on the west of the country, lost out. Between 1966 and 1977, 350 factories closed or moved elsewhere. By 1978, Liverpool had the highest unemployment rate in the country. In the 1980s things got worse. By 1981, 20 per cent of the city's workforce were unemployed and 'it was reported that there were just 49 jobs on offer for 13,505 youngsters registered as unemployed' (Murden, 2006, 428). As du Noyer states 'the 1980s saw Liverpool's old fame replaced by infamy. Suddenly this was Bad News Town. Somebody dubbed it the Museum of Horrifying Example' (du Noyer, 2004, 174). Such was the sense of dereliction that an American band, 'The Bangles', released a cover version of a song where the chorus repeated 'I'm going down to Liverpool to do nothing all the days of my life'.

As in the rest of the country, there was opposition. The local council in Liverpool was for a period in the 1980s at loggerheads with the government. Liverpool was also the scene of the Toxteth riots in 1981. Touted as race riots, they were as much to do with unemployment and police harassment as they were to do with race. Thatcher's response to these in her memoirs is telling of her thinking.

'I had been told that some of the young people got into trouble through boredom and not having enough to do,' she wrote 'But you had only to look at the grounds around those houses with the grass untended, some of it waist high, and the litter, to see that this was a false analysis. They had plenty of constructive things to do if they wanted. Instead, I asked myself how people could live in such circumstances without trying to clear up the mess.'

THATCHER quoted in Marr, 2008, 390

Subsequently, Government papers, released in 2011, bear out the attitude of some people in Thatcher's government towards the city, urging her to abandon it to managed decline. In the words of du Noyer, '[t]he Beat City became the Beaten City' (du Noyer, 2004, 175).

Theatrical context: Andrew Lloyd Webber

Michael Billington recounts a story of Peter Hall, then director of the National Theatre, being told off by Mrs Thatcher for complaining about the state of British Theatre. She pointed out to him that British theatre was famous the world over. 'Look,' Billington reports she triumphantly said, 'at Andrew Lloyd Webber' (Billington, 2007, 284).

Andrew Lloyd Webber was everywhere in the 1980s. Alongside the theatre producer, Cameron Mackintosh, who was responsible for Schoenberg and Boublil's *Les Miserables* (1985) and *Miss Saigon* (1989), he dominated and defined British theatre. Although he had started working in the 1970s (his first major success was *Jesus Christ Superstar* in 1972), the 1980s produced a string of hugely successful shows: *Cats* (1981), *Starlight Express* (1984) and *Phantom of the Opera* (1986). *Cats,* a 'statistic-busting phenomenon' went on to run in London's West End for twenty-one years, being performed in thirty countries and seen by over 75 million people (Billington, 2007, 288). *The Phantom of the Opera*, according to the show's website, has been seen by over 140 million people in 151 cities and taken in excess of $6 billion (the highest grossing film to date, *Avatar*, took $2.7 billion).

The musical was the dominant theatrical form of the decade and in particular the megamusical, big in the scale of the story, enormous in the scale of the spectacle on stage. The lack of dialogue (these were mostly musicals that were sung all the way through) meant that they had global appeal and could be exported worldwide, like Coca-Cola and Levi's Jeans, crossing barriers of language and culture. These musicals, argues Billington, offered the audiences 'both escape from social reality and spiritual uplift' and 'ultimately turned into the theatrical equivalent of multinational companies. In their wealth making capacity and corporatism, musicals were the perfect expression of Thatcherite values' (Billington, 2007, 286). The link to Thatcherite values of the individual can be seen clearly in *Starlight Express*. The show revolves around a race to become the fastest engine in the world between Rusty (a steam train relegated to the sidings), Electra (an electric train) and Greaseball (a diesel train). As Rusty hits rock bottom, thinking he will win neither the race nor the heart of

Pearl, the mystical force of the title is revealed and Rusty discovers that he himself is the magical Starlight Express. Faith in himself restored, he goes on to win both the race and Pearl.

Musicals in the 1980s, as Michael Billington suggests, served a dual function: to 'distract us from the daily realities of Thatcher's Britain while exemplifying the pursuit of profit that was its guiding principle' (Billington, 2007, 294). They were stories of nineteenth-century opera houses, the Vietnam War via Puccini's opera *Madame Butterfly* and cats going up to heaven. *Blood Brothers,* with its local accents and setting, with its implied critique of Thatcherism and without any roller skates or crashing chandeliers, represents a very different kind of work as Peter Taylor's review of the show suggests.

> Emerging during the decade that landed us with *Cats* and *Starlight Express*, *Blood Brothers* was always something of an anomaly as an Eighties musical. It dealt with ordinary recognised people for a start, rather than a ménage of poetic moggies or a set of singing choo-choos. It was on a humane scale too, you did not go out humming the lavish set and the budget.
>
> TAYLOR, 1998

Theatrical context: Liverpool

In the programme for the original West End transfer of the show, playwright Bill Morrison, who was working with Willy Russell at Liverpool Playhouse at the time, described *Blood Brothers* as 'a new sound from an old history'. He cites the Mersey poets, Roger McGough, Adrian Henri and Brian Patten who took the poem off the page, stood up and told the story. After them, music was added to the words by The Beatles and both of these influenced the kind of work being produced at Liverpool's Everyman Theatre where Willy Russell started out as a playwright in the 1970s. Here work was made that had a firm local commitment, an abundance of music and an informal and lively style of presentation. He also locates Willy Russell's work in an oral tradition, stories that are passed on by word of mouth rather than written down. 'In the same way as the poets stood up and lifted the poem off the literary page', he concludes, 'he has reaffirmed theatre as rich spoken and sung language – it is the robust lyricism of ordinary people.' To Bill Morrison's context should also be added the rich history of folk music in Liverpool (at the peak of its revival in the 1960s there were 72 folk clubs in the city), of which Willy Russell was a part in the 1960s with his band Kirkby Town Three.

Things to do

- Pick a scene from the play and write down what you would need to change to update it to the present day. Take a couple of examples you have noted down and rewrite some of the play's dialogue and stage directions accordingly.

- Choose a city that you have experience and/or knowledge of and consider how *Blood Brothers* would need to be adapted if it was set there.

Themes

Fate and destiny

The final question the narrator puts to the audience asks if we blame superstition or class for the tragedy, highlighting both of these as main themes. Both can be connected with a sense of destiny or fate and the structure of the play, in which we see where events will end up at the start, suggests a strong sense of the inevitable or the unalterable. Things have to be like this and there is nothing that can change them. Superstition too suggests a belief in predetermination. If you put new shoes on the table or see a lone magpie, something bad will happen. Some ways of understanding class suggest that there is an inevitability about your life because of the class you are born into. So both superstition and class are connected in *Blood Brothers* to questions of destiny and there is a strong sense of fatalism in the play. Things could not have happened differently. Or could they? Russell does not blame any one character for what happens but there are moments where if characters acted differently, fate could have been changed. While class and a belief in superstition are key here, individual responsibility also has its place.

Believing in superstition

It is the narrator who reminds us throughout about superstitions from the shoes on the table and salt being spilt to breaking mirrors and walking on pavement cracks. However, it is Mrs Johnstone who first mentions them. As Mrs Lyons puts her shopping on the table, she is horrified, stopping mid-sentence to explain that you never put new shoes on the table because 'you never know what'll happen' but in response to being asked if she is superstitious, she claims she is not (33).

Not all the characters in the play believe in superstitions. At the outset, the Lyons family reject them. When Mrs Johnstone tells Edward to go home before the bogey man gets him, he has no idea what she means by the phrase and has to look it up in the dictionary. Mrs Lyons is damning of a 'silly' mother who would use that phrase and adamant that there is no such thing. But as the influence of the Johnstone's becomes apparent on Edward, he starts to believe in superstitions telling his mother not to look at a magpie because it stands for sorrow. Mrs Lyons still condemns superstition as the kind of silly thing that Mickey said but she has already shown that she too is starting to believe. She stops mid-sentence as her husband puts a pair of shoes on the table and rushes to sweep them off. Her conversion can be seen to come from a sense of fear and foreboding. 'If we stay here I feel that something terrible will happen', she tells her husband, echoing Mrs Johnstone's comment to her (68). She becomes a figure very like the bogey man herself, the mad woman who lives on the hill and scares the children. Of all the characters, Mr Lyons presents himself as the most rational, consistently refusing to to get taken in by 'stupid superstition' (75).

There are other references woven into the play to superstitions. The number seven recurs from Mrs Johnstone's seven children – to the seven years between each age the twins appear and Mickey being sentenced to seven years in prison. It is often seen as a lucky number but there are seven deadly sins and a broken mirror means seven years bad luck. Superstition is also connected with religion; Mrs Johnstone is made to swear on the bible and the 'thing' was done 'in the name of Jesus' (39). There is also a suggestion that Mrs Johnstone is Catholic (she dances with a picture of the Pope). Russell's argument here is to question people's *belief* in superstition (and by inference religion) as something both powerful and dangerous.

Is superstition to blame? There is an argument to be made that if Mrs Johnstone had not believed in Mrs Lyons' concocted story about twins being separated then none of the ensuing events would have happened, but it is only one side of the question being asked of us at the end.

Class or nature v nurture

Class is a complex idea. What is easier to say is that class affects how people are able to live their lives. It impacts on where you live, how you speak, the opportunities and education you have, the work you do. It can also be seen to impact on the way you behave. Edward, for example, is polite (Mrs Johnstone imagines how a child brought up in the Lyons house would not fight or be found 'effin' and blindin'') (38).

In *Blood Brothers*, the impact of class is key and the classes are seen to be in opposition to each other. It is possible to develop this and see the issue of class as analogous to a divided nation, a point Irving Wardle makes, arguing Blood Brothers is 'a fable of the two nations represented here' (Wardle, 1983). The implications can be seen in the comparison between Mrs Johnstone and Mrs Lyons, obvious from early on. They are both instantly recognizable class stereotypes (see the section on dramatic structure for how this works in terms of language and costume). Mrs Johnstone has to go to work whereas there is no mention of Mrs Lyons working. Instead she can afford to employ a cleaner. Mrs Johnstone is warm hearted; Mrs Lyons is cold. Mrs Johnstone lives in a terraced house and then on an estate; Mrs Lyons lives in a large house by the park and then in a house on top of the hill. These differences can then be seen to play out in the lives of the twins, in particular at school. Edward is at private boarding school where he is 'doing very well' and goes on to university (88). Mickey's school is a Secondary Modern[1] which is *all boredom and futility*' (89). Here, he does not learn anything that will be useful for him when he leaves and the expectation is that he will immediately get a job. Edward, it is suggested (because he can find Mickey and Linda a house) has a well-paid management job. Mickey ends up with a manual job making-up boxes.

Class also impacts on how people are treated. The most obvious example of this is the response of the policeman to the parents. Confronting Mrs Johnstone, he threatens her with having to appear in court again, insistent that it was a serious crime. 'There'll be no more bloody warnings from now on', he tells her (71). With the Lyons family, he shares a glass of scotch, calls Edward a good lad and Mr Lyons sir and sees the misdemeanor as 'more of a prank', suggesting that Mr Lyons docks his pocket money. 'Make sure he keeps with his own kind', he advises, suggesting he thinks Mickey is to blame (72).

Alongside questions about the impact of class, *Blood Brothers* also raises questions about whether nature (genetic

---

[1] Comprehensive schools were established between 1965 and 1975. Until then there were Grammar schools if you passed an examination at 11 or Secondary Modern schools if you failed.

make-up) or nurture (upbringing) defines a person's chances in life. Twins are seen to be genetically identical, so differences between them will be down to their upbringing. However, it is worth remembering that this may only be the case where twins are identical (genetics is a complex and still developing area of science). Fraternal twins (i.e. twins who are not identical) do not share the same genes; there are many examples of twins who are a boy and a girl who clearly do not share the same genes. In *Blood Brothers*, we know they are twins but not if they are identical but there are moments that suggest nature defines your life, in particular Edward's growing affinity with Mrs Johnstone, his natural mother. By contrast, his relationship with his adoptive mother becomes increasingly distant. He also becomes increasingly like Mickey as their friendship develops, talking back to his mother and adopting the language used by his twin, saying hi-ya instead of hello. This could suggest him reverting to his natural state and his seemingly natural affinity with Mickey alongside Mrs Lyons' assertion that he is 'drawn' to 'these people' adds weight to an argument about the importance of nature (68–9).

Mickey's final cry of 'I could have been him' suggests that he had the potential to have been like Edward if he had been given different life (or class) chances (129). It is an idea reflected by Billington's review which suggests 'the moral is blindingly clear that environment counts for more than heredity and that class-structure divides natural kin' (Billington, 1983). Nurture is more important than nature.

But will having money make you happy?

People suffer in *Blood Brothers* because they do not have money. 'Ey, Mother, I'm starvin' an' there's nothin' in', complains one of the Johnstone children (31). Mrs Johnstone's response is to promise the kids they will 'live like kings' and 'bright young things' when she brings 'home the dough' (32). Children cannot, she knows 'live on love alone' (35). So, does

Blood Brothers suggest that money (or having stuff) will bring you happiness?

Money does, at the start, equate with power. Mrs Lyons has power over Mrs Johnstone because she pays her wages and can give her a week off work on full pay. She uses her wealth to persuade Mrs Johnstone to give her the baby and uses money to try and solve her problems. She can afford to move her family away and she can afford to try and bribe Mrs Johnstone to move again. When Edward offers Mickey money at Christmas he seems to think, like his mother, that money can solve problems. For the working class characters, on the other hand, the lack of money makes them powerless. Mrs Johnstone cannot afford to keep both twins and has to accept Mrs Lyons' proposition.

At the same time, money does not always seem to be the answer. The kids may be hungry but the lack of money does not stop them from using their imagination and playing games together. By contrast, Edward, who has money, is lonely. Nor does Edward's money stop him having the same adolescent problems as Mickey. He too does not know what to say to girls and he too is worried about bad breath and eyes that do not match. Nor can money buy back his blood brother. Mrs Lyons is not made happy by money and cannot buy her way out of trouble and unhappiness. She also thinks that her promise of all the good things in life for her son (even silver trays to have his meals on) will make him love her, but it does not.

This does not mean that getting money and things is not a temptation. Mrs Johnstone is taken in by the things in the catalogue even though she knows she cannot afford them. Sammy goes from trying to save some money on his bus fare to violent robbery. Mickey, desperate for money, is persuaded to join him by the thought of where he could take Linda if he 'had cash like that' (116). But, the pursuit of money and stuff means there is always a price to be paid. Mrs Johnstone has to watch as her things are repossessed. Sammy and Mickey both end up in prison. In the end, money might equate with power but it does not bring happiness and everyone's lives are in tatters at the conclusion.

Dreaming of escape

Jaspar Rees claims that 'no one understands escapism like Willy Russell', and many of his plays contain characters who try to escape (or dream of escaping) although they are often prevented by other people (Rees, 2010). In *Blood Brothers,* although there is a strong sense of fate, this does not stop people dreaming of a better life and wanting to escape or dreaming of being someone different. Mrs Johnstone lives much of her life in a fantasy world. She spins dreams of food for the children, conjuring up pictures of ham and jam and spam and even milkshake for the baby (31). She dreams of a new home where nobody has heard of them, where the washing stays clean on the line and where she will have a front room for best so that if the Pope happens to fly in from Rome he can eat toast and drink tea with her. From this last aspiration we can see that her bright new day has little relationship to reality and although she does go dancing with the milkman (and gets asked out by the judge), as soon as they arrive in the country things start to go wrong. Sammy climbs on a cow which turns out to be a bull, Donna Marie steps in something nasty and it is not long before Sammy is in trouble for burning down the school. Such reality checks do little to stop her dreaming and at the end of the play, she is still asking the audience to tell her that the whole story is just a dream. Mrs Lyons dreams too. Firstly of a child and then of moving away from the people she thinks are drawing Edward away from her. As with Mrs Johnstone, her dreams of escape do not work. None of the dreaming seems to help the characters really escape.

Other characters have their dreams of change too. Edward and Mickey dream about being more like each other. Edward dreams of Linda loving him, of bringing her flowers and taking her on trips to the sea. Linda dreams that everything will be alright when Mickey gets a job and they get a house and she dreams about the possibility of becoming 'the girl inside the woman' again (123). There are, the narrator tells us, moments in life when 'everything is possible', the world's within your reach if only 'we didn't live in life, as well as dreams' (106). Living is different to dreaming. The broken bottles are still in the sand, the oil is in the water and while you may have a moment when 'you can't understand/How living could be anything other than a dream', real life soon reappears (106).

Childhood, growing up and friendship

As children, the twins are determined to stay friends despite the obstacles put in their paths. They bridge their class differences in a way that indicates things could be different, suggesting there is something to celebrate about the openness of the young or to regret about the acquired prejudice of their parents.

They very quickly and seemingly naturally become firm friends, blood brothers. When Sammy derides Edward by calling him 'a poshy', Mickey declares 'he's my best friend' and their childhood is shown as a carefree time of games and sharing sweets (55). Almost until the end, they then stick together, despite the adults best efforts to keep them apart. Mrs Johnstone forbids Mickey from playing near the park and tells Edward to 'beat it' (57). Mrs Lyons insists it is Edward's bedtime when Mickey comes to see if he can play. She then tells Edward never to go where boys like that live because he is not the same as them. Edward does not understand this idea at all. In fact, he tells his mother that he likes Mickey more than her (the boys are united in both thinking that their mothers are mad). In an attempt to finally separate them, Mrs Lyons moves, but even this fails. Mickey manages to get some money to visit him on the bus (and in a poor family that suggests a commitment from him) but does not know where to go. They find each other once again, their second meeting mirroring the first as Mickey replaces the demand for a sweet with a demand for a cigarette, staying close friends throughout their childhood and adolescence.

It is only when they are adults, when Edward comes back from university and Mickey has lost his job, that the rift appears and the adult Mickey tells Edward to 'piss off' (115). Where once they stood together, now they wear different shoes. 'In your shoes, I'd be the same', Mickey tells Edward, but 'I am not in your shoes. I'm in these looking at you' (115). The scene, with Mickey throwing the money he is offered to the ground, echoes an earlier scene suggesting that they have both become like their mothers and are no longer the children able to bridge the gaps. 'Go on . . . beat it,' Mickey tells Edward, 'before I hit y'' (115). Edward slowly backs away. Adulthood leads Mickey to reject Edward.

Secrets, lies, deceit and guilt

There are many different kinds of lies that people tell and many different reasons for people telling lies – and untruths run throughout the play with almost all the characters telling lies or having secrets. Linda does not tell Mickey (or Mrs Johnstone) who has sorted out the house and the job. Mickey and Linda lie to Edward about saying dead 'funny things' to the police (67). Edward will not tell his mother where he has got the locket from or why he wears it. 'It's a secret', he tells her, echoing the words Mrs Johnstone said when she gave it to him. 'It's just a secret, everybody has secrets, don't you have secrets?' (92).

There is one big lie that runs through the heart of *Blood Brothers,* a lie shared by the audience that is only revealed to Mickey and Edward at the very end of the play. It colours the whole play leading to more and more lies being told, snowballing until the two brothers find themselves caught in a web of falsehoods that leaves them feeling guilty and, in the case of Mrs Lyons, eaten up by deceit and mistrust. Mrs Johnstone cannot tell her children the truth when she comes back from the hospital with only one child, although her story that he is in heaven and has everything he wants is not far from the truth. Mrs Lyons cannot tell the truth about why she wants £50 from her husband or about why she wants to move. It is her distrust of Mrs Johnstone, her refusal to believe that she is not following her, that leads her to go mad, to try and stab Mrs Johnstone and then to tell Mickey about Edward and Linda. In the end, it is only when the truth comes out that the tragedy unfolds in the moment that Mrs Johnstone tells Mickey that they are brothers. So, it is possible to argue that it is lies and deceit rather than class or superstition that causes the death of the twins.

Motifs

Dancing

Dancing is usually associated with being happy and there are many references in the play where dancing is associated with happiness. Mrs Johnstone, in particular, dances when she is happy. It is associated with her as a young woman meeting her husband. It is associated with her joy at being told she has a new house when she dances with a picture of the Pope and dreams of gentlemen friends taking her dancing to local bands. She is so happy to get her job with Mrs Lyons – that we see her dancing to work, acquiring a brush, dusters and mop on the way and she is clearly glad to see Edward again when, as the boys go off to the cinema, she is left lilting '*the "We Go Dancing" line*' (100). For both Mickey and Edward, dancing is a sign of affection; they want to dance with the people they love. Yet, these are fleeting moments of happiness. Mrs Johnstone's husband leaves her to dance with someone else, she loses her job and in the moments after her delight at seeing Edward again, Mrs Lyons bursts into the kitchen and tries to stab her.

There are also references to dancing which are not quite so cheerful. The image of the awkward fourteen-year-old Edward being taught by his mother to waltz stands in stark contrast to Mickey's secret dancing or Edward's joyful grabbing of Linda's mate who he waltzes round the street while singing 'Tits, tits, tits . . .' (102). There is also a darker inference in the reference to Linda and Edward dancing as friends and to Mickey's invitation to his wife to get dressed up because he is going to take her dancing. As the play moves towards its conclusion, dancing stops being a measure of happiness and becomes a representation of something darker. In prison, Mickey's mind has gone dancing and there is 'no cause for dancing' suggesting there will be no more happiness, however short-lived it might be (121).

Marilyn Monroe

The image of Marilyn Monroe, which adorned the gauze[2] for the first production of the musical, is woven throughout the play connecting to both Mrs Johnstone and Mickey and tracing their lives in a reflection of her own. Her importance as a symbol is suggested by the fact that the first full song is called 'Marilyn Monroe' and her name is the last thing heard in the show. Her image is used in two main ways. At times, she represents sexiness, lovely legs, bright young things – and the kind of girl Mickey dreams about at night. Towards the end of the play, the references become darker. In prison, Mickey 'treats his ills with daily pills' and looks so old '[y]ou'd think he was dead' – both like Marilyn Monroe (120–1).

Marilyn Monroe has come to represent both of these things. On the one hand she is the blonde bombshell, a world famous, glamorous sex symbol, vivacious, irresistible, a fantasy woman. Mrs Johnstone is flattered to be compared to her by her husband and the judge and, on stage, the opening glimpse of Mrs Johnstone often echoes the iconography of Marilyn Monroe. But on the other hand, however, there is a darker side to her story. She was also a tragic figure who lived a short and troubled life, dying at the age of thirty-six from an overdose of barbiturates in circumstances that are still open to speculation. Despite her success, she suffered from depression and was addicted to prescription drugs. Lee Strasberg, her acting tutor (also famous for teaching The Method School of acting in America) summed up her contradictory qualities describing her as having a 'luminous quality', a 'combination of wistfulness, radiance and yearning' that made everyone want to 'share in the childish naiveté which was at once so shy and

---

[2] A gauze is a transparent curtain sometimes hung at the front of the stage. When it is lit from the front it is opaque but when it is lit from behind, it becomes transparent.

yet so vibrant' (Strasberg quoted in Harding, 2012, 144). Like Mickey, her life was shaped by the world she found herself in and the role she was expected to play and like Mickey, it did not end well. Mrs Johnstone's return to Marilyn Monroe in the final song reflects those dreams that came to nothing.

Guns

Alongside a catapult and two knives, guns and shooting are liberally littered throughout the play, moving from toys to real guns in the hands of Sammy and the police. When Mickey first appears, he has a toy gun and is complaining that Sammy has stolen his best gun. The first time Sammy appears, he is pointing a gun at the twins, complaining that it is 'last' because it only fires caps and boasting that he is going to get a real gun (or at least an air gun). The big gun moment in Act One is the children's game where they start with guns and end with bombs that can 'destroy ze 'emisphere' (in reality a condom full of water) (63). We know this is a game, because the children tell us and because there are rules; as long as you have your fingers crossed and you count from one to ten, you can get up again. It is an innocent game but it prefigures events to come. When a gun appears again, it is an air pistol in the park. The guns are starting to get more real and this time it lands them in trouble with the police. Whilst guns, particularly in Sammy's hands, suggest increasing violence and danger, guns in Linda's hands have a different connotation. When she is seven, and one of the lads, she can fire a gun hitting the target. When she is sixteen and more conscious of being a woman her skill diminishes and in the funfair she cannot hit anything.

There are two big gun moments in Act Two. The first is the robbery. This time, as Sammy tells us, 'it's not a toy' and 'we're not playing games. You don't get up if one of these hits you', although he refers to the gun as a shooter as if he is in a film (118). This gun leaves a man bleeding on the floor. The second moment uses the same gun retrieved by Mickey from under the floorboards where Sammy has hidden it. He cannot manage to shoot Edward and it is only when Mrs Johnstone tells him the truth that as he waves the gun at Edward, it explodes. In response, the police open fire and four guns kill him. The final moment happens very quickly and without any words, underlining the senselessness and waste that guns produce.

Things to do

- Pick out a moment in the play where you feel a character is entirely responsible for their own actions and write down your reasons for thinking so. Let a classmate read what you have written and invite him or her to provide counter-arguments.

- Twins often feature in stage, television and cinema productions. Can you think of any examples? How do they compare to Russell's presentation of twins?

Character

Mickey

Mickey first appears at the age of seven, knocking incessantly at his front door, a lively, imaginative and streetwise boy who knows his mother does not want to see the rent man. He tells her excitedly about the three thousand dead Indians and why it was their fault that he had ended up playing by the park. He is daring. Cutting his hand to swear the oath, he tells Edward, 'It hurts you know.' (54). There is a sense of fun, adventure and mischief about him. With Linda, he encourages Edward to cheek the policeman when they get caught throwing stones (although the inference is that neither of them have ever told a policeman their name was Adolf Hitler). Alongside his energy and wit, he is also sensitive. He seems close to his mother, noticing she is happy when they move. Taunted by the gang, he cries, and he cries several times during the play.

From the start he is lost and lonely, despite living in a big family. Left outside to play by himself, he is '*desultory*' wishing he was Sammy (50). Later, on a long Sunday afternoon, he misses Edward and wishes he was more like him. When Edward does present himself as a friend, Mickey accepts the friendship quickly and within a short space of time they are swearing to always stand by each other. During the rest of the play Mickey is happiest when Edward is there.

As a teenager, Mickey is self-conscious, not confident about his appearance nor about Linda. Embarrassed by his mother's teasing and Linda's declarations of love, he cannot articulate his own feelings about her to her face. It is only when he is alone he can admit that he wants to kiss her and put his arms around her and 'even fornicate with y'' (94). But, as his friendship with Edward is re-born, the old Mickey reappears. He teases Edward about girlfriends and shamelessly tries to persuade his mother they are going to see a travelogue about Sweden. The old gang is back together and the happiest section of the play shows the summers spent together as they grow from fourteen to eighteen. Finally, they do all cheek the policeman with Edward sitting on top of the lamp post and their time is filled with the fairground, talking the night away outside the chip shop and taking silly photographs. Mickey's fear of asking Linda out is even overcome, with some prompting from Edward.

This is brought up short as Winter breaks 'the promise that Summer had just made' (110). Torn apart from Edward once again who is off to university, Mickey is left with a pregnant girlfriend and a job in a factory making cardboard boxes. He gets married, loses his job, loses his blood brother and he falls apart, the promise of the lively seven-year-old lost to the realities of grown-up life. Edward, protected by money and university, is still a child, bouncing back home at Christmas ready for parties and booze. In their penultimate meeting, Mickey wishes he could still believe in 'all that blood brother stuff' but he cannot 'because while no one was looking I grew up'. It was all just 'kids' stuff' (115). All of his hopes and dreams

have been taken away from him by life. He agrees to help
Sammy – because he wants to take Linda out dancing for New
Year. In prison, he succumbs to depression and pills, telling
Linda afterwards that he needs them so he can be invisible.
When he fears that Linda, the only thing he thinks he has left,
is being taken away from him, everything unravels and he sets
out to confront Edward. By now, he has stopped taking the
tablets and has begun thinking again. What he sees is very clear
to him, as he asks Edward, 'how come you got everything . . .
an' I got nothin'?' (128). It is a question answered for him by
his mother and Mickey's final howl of rage – suggests his life
need not have been as it was. It is a plea which begins '*deep
down inside him*': 'You! (*Screaming*) You! Why didn't you give
me away! (*He stands glaring at her, almost uncontrollable with
rage.*) I could have been . . . I could have been him!' (129).

Edward

Edward is Mickey's opposite. The boys' sense of this is clear in
'My Friend', each wishing they could be more like each other,
conscious that the other is better at things they cannot do (an
idea revisited later in 'That Guy'). Edward admires Mickey
because he can swear like a soldier and makes him laugh with
his stories and runs around with dirty knees. He appears in
front of Mickey just as he is bemoaning the fact that he is not
more like Sammy, offering Mickey an alternative to his brother.
He is '*bright and forthcoming*', immediately offering sweets
when asked, suggesting an openness and generosity (51). Later,
he offers to get Mickey cigarettes, gives him the toy gun his
father has bought him and when he comes back from university
to find Mickey has lost his job, he offers him money. Unlike
Mickey's laughing and swearing, Edward giggles and says
'super fun' and 'smashing' (52). He is well-mannered, surprising
Mrs Johnstone by asking how she is. 'I don't usually have kids
enquiring about my health', she explains, calling him Master
Lyons (73). He is educated, knows he can look up words in a

dictionary and goes to a boarding school and later to university. The play never says which university he goes to, but his teacher talks of Oxbridge (the entrance examination to go to either Oxford or Cambridge) and his friends visiting at Christmas have names like Baz and Ronnie and call him 'Lyo' and 'Lyonese' suggesting a high-class university. He is, in Sammy's words, 'a friggin' poshy', living firstly in a house by the park and then in the house on the top of the hill (55).

He is also innocent. When Sammy is demanding sweets, Mickey is urgently suggesting they do not have any. Edward immediately says that they do and that he has given one to Mickey for Sammy. He falls for the story about standing up to the policeman and when Mrs Johnstone says she has been trying to move for years, he innocently asks, 'Why don't you buy a new house near us?' (74). Later in the play, he shows his naivety by asking Mickey why a job is so important. If he could not get a job, he would 'draw the dole, live like a bohemian, tilt my hat to the world and say "screw you"', he tells him (115). He can talk in this way because he is protected from the real world by his money and, although he is the same age as Mickey, this has allowed him to remain innocent and childlike.

Yet, while he is disconnected from the harsh realities of the world, he can also stand up for himself. When his mother refuses to let him play with Mickey, he accuses her of not loving him, saying he prefers Mickey and calling her a 'fuckoff' (60). When the teacher demands his locket he refuses suggesting he should 'take a flying fuck at a rolling doughnut' and then refuses to tell his mother who gave it to him. His use of the 'F word' at both these moments suggests the influence of Mickey, an influence that can also be seen by him smoking after they come out of the cinema.

Edward does end up, it is suggested, with a good job and as a local councillor, having enough influence to organize a job and a house for Mickey. Yet, while he has material possessions, he is not necessarily happy. His loneliness as a boy is apparent when he goes to say goodbye to Mrs Johnstone. Crying, he tells her he does not want to go but wants to 'stay here where my friends are ... where Mickey is' (73). He is no better equipped at dealing with girls than Mickey and his advice on what to say to girls is gained from reading books not from his own experience. He is confined by his mother, his life lacks warmth, he does not marry the girl he loves and in the end he is estranged from his best friend.

The narrator

Irving Wardle described the narrator as a 'satanic figure' who punctuates the action 'with fearful references to lone magpies, new shoes on the table and the fateful secret known only to the two women' (1983). He does seem to be a sinister character, constantly reminding us that things will not end well and there is no escape He raises the tension, telling us the devil is closing in; he is 'gonna find y–' (48), he is 'creeping down the hall' (48), he has 'moved in down the street from you', maybe 'even leanin' on your door' (97) until he is right beside you, 'screamin' deep inside you' (126). He is the only unnamed character, the only one to speak in verse, setting him apart. He stands outside the action, a brooding presence, eyes like a hawk, watching. He talks directly to no other character and no-one talks to him or seems aware of his presence. Dressed in a dark suit in the stage productions (although this is not indicated in the play text) gives him a neutral status but also means he is appropriately dressed for the end, as if he always knows that the play will end with a funeral. He often helps orchestrate things on stage, moving props to ensure the show runs smoothly as if he is in control, arranging what is happening.

The actor playing the narrator also plays other characters from the outside world, all of whom bring bad news, as if the world is conspiring to make life even more difficult. The milkman tells Mrs Johnstone 'no money, no milk' (31). The gynaecologist tells her she is expecting twins. The bus conductor ensures Sammy is handed over to the police. The teachers are the cause of the twins being suspended. In bringing bad news, these characters also appear indifferent; 'it's got nothin' to do with me' claims the milkman (31).

For all these reasons, it would be simple to read him as a satanic character as indifferent to the fate of the twins as the milkman. But while he might remind the characters (and the audience) that bad things will happen, that 'a debt is a debt, and must be paid', this is different to equating him with the devil (40). As a character that stands outside of the action, there is a neutrality about him. He is reminiscent of the chorus in Ancient Greek tragedies providing background information to help the audience follow the story and commenting on the themes and the characters. He fills in moments of action ('There's a man lies bleeding on a garage floor' (118)) and keeps us in touch with time passing as the children grow up. Or he fills in subtext, telling us, for example, what Mrs Lyons is thinking when Mrs Johnstone tells her she is expecting twins. In a play that is episodic, he also serves as a linking device that runs throughout, holding the play together, starting and finishing it and reminding us that it is a story. He confronts the audience with questions about the play and characters, making us think about what is happening, asking us to 'judge for ourselves' how Mrs Johnstone came to be a 'mother so cruel' (29). At the end, he frames the key question the play asks: 'And do we blame superstition for what came to pass?/Or could it be what we, the English, have come to know as class?' (129). The fact that this question comes from him and that he is an almost constant presence throughout suggests that he is both important and serves a more complex function than simply being the portentous and dark heart of the play.

Mrs Johnstone

The narrator sets up the audience's expectations of Mrs Johnstone as a 'mother so cruel' with 'a stone in place of her heart' (29). Yet this judgement of her seems to be at odds with the character presented in the play. He does ask the audience to judge how she came to play this part suggesting that she has not always been like this but little in her character seems to live up to this description.

From the start, it is apparent that Mrs Johnstone's life is hard. By the time she is twenty-five (and looking much older), she has seven children and her husband leaves her pregnant with the twins. There is never enough money. She cannot even pay the milkman but a hard life has not made her uncaring. She is presented throughout as a warm, easy going character with a sense of fun. This is seen, for example, when she affectionately teases her fourteen-year-old son about being in love with Linda, joking with him that he has been talking about her in his sleep. As Linda appears, she continues to tease, asking if he is waiting for his mother to give him 'a big sloppy kiss' (85). Her natural ebullience and optimism bubbles over when she finds they are moving and she always seems to make the best of things. Even when the new house does not solve all of her problems, she stays positive. The neighbours might fight on Saturday night but 'never in the week' (82). There is a softness about her, especially in relation to her children. She makes excuses for Sammy burning down the school. She cannot part with Edward without giving him the locket as a memento.

There is a marked contrast between her and Mrs Lyons in relation to their children. When Mrs Lyons teaches Edward to dance she is clinging, fussy and holds onto him, asking him for reassurance. In contrast, when the boys try to hide from Mrs Johnstone which film they are going to see, she is much more relaxed and broadminded, joking with them, leading Edward to tell Mickey, 'She's fabulous your ma, isn't she?' (99). Despite all her good humour, she is not always very responsible. Glen Walford describes her as being 'a fantasist' who does not live in the real world. She buys things on credit, overwhelmed by how nice things look in the shop, even though she knows she does not have the money to pay for them. Within two pages of having had her wireless repossessed, she is promising her fretful children that they can look in the catalogue the following week for a bicycle.

Such childish behaviour is at odds with her role in the play as a mother (in the original version of the show, the character – was simply called The Mother). Whilst Mrs Lyons cannot have children, she 'can't stop havin'' them' (33). Despite having so many children she 'loves the bones of every one of them' and despite her childishness, she is also a character who changes during the play (9). In her final confrontation with Mrs Lyons, she refuses to take the money having learned that she would only buy more stuff with it. Instead, she wants to keep the life she has made out in the country. 'It's not much of one,' she tells the irate Mrs Lyons, 'but I made it. I'm stayin' here. You move if you want to' (101).

She could be seen as a cruel mother because she gives away her baby but her reasons seem to be unselfish. She is moved by Mrs Lyons' desperate need for a child and by the thought that her child will have a better life, and she is scared of The Welfare who are already threatening to take her children away. Her distress at giving one twin away when Mrs Lyons arrives to collect the baby is apparent; she begs for a few more days with both of them and then cannot bear to hear which one is being taken. 'Don't tell me which one', she says to Mrs Lyons. 'Just take him, take him' (43). She tries to stick by the agreement and keep the twins apart but cannot and, finally, does not stop the boys becoming friends. At the end, she frantically rushes to the Town Hall to try and stop Mickey, the end being more tragic because of our sympathy for Mrs Johnstone.

Mrs Lyons

Mrs Lyons is presented as the opposite of Mrs Johnstone. While Mrs Johnstone cannot stop getting pregnant and lives surrounded by the affectionate squabbling of her children, Mrs Lyons lives by herself in a large house while her husband is away working. She is unable to have children of her own. And there is much that might point to Mrs Lyons being the villain. One of the first things she does is to put her new shoes on the table, breaking a superstition and starting a train of events which ends with the death of the twins. She persuades Mrs Johnstone to allow her to have one of the twins, exploiting Mrs Johnstone's poverty to get what she wants. She is very much in control at the outset, issuing commands, like 'they shall be raised apart and never, ever told what was once the truth' and expecting to be obeyed (47). She is also manipulative. Exploiting the fact that she knows Mrs Johnstone is superstitious, she fabricates the story of separated twins dying if they find out the truth and she shows she has no concern for the feelings of others. Having promised Mrs Johnstone she will be able to see her son every day at work, she very soon afterwards sacks her. She also lies to her husband about why she wants to get rid of Mrs Johnstone and deceives him into thinking it is his child.

As the play progresses, she becomes increasingly fearful that the truth will surface and she will lose Edward, persuading her husband that they have to move. She is possessive and over-protective of Edward, not wanting him to play out and she becomes insecure, seeking reassurance from Edward that they have had a good time in the holidays. Gradually she becomes more and more paranoid, convinced that Mrs Johnstone is following her, convinced that she has given Edward the locket so he will not forget her. In the end, she firmly believes that Mrs Johnstone has ruined her. While she starts by believing an adopted child can 'become one's own', by the end she is sure that when Edward was a tiny baby 'I'd see him looking straight at me and I'd think, he knows' (33; 100). She tries to buy off Mrs Johnstone again, offering her money to move away, and when she refuses, Mrs Lyons lunges at her with a kitchen knife cursing her and calling her a witch. In reality, it is Mrs Lyons who becomes the witch, a madwoman living on the hill scaring children, their chant (coming from off-stage) sounding as if it is echoing in her own head. Her final appearance is to show

Mickey that Linda and Edward are together. She says nothing, just points out what is happening to him, a broken woman, beyond speech.

Whilst there is a lot of evidence in the play that she is a 'bad' character there is also more to her character. In the scene where she persuades Mrs Johnstone to give her the baby, there is a very different Mrs Lyons. She is lonely. She has wanted to adopt a child but is prevented by Mr Lyons who wants his own son. When she hatches her plan to take one of the twins, she is excited and happy, believing she is helping Mrs Johnstone out. 'It's mad,' she tells Mrs Johnstone, '. . . but it's wonderful, it's perfect' (36). The song, 'My Child' shows her real loneliness and her dream of having a child, a child she promises Mrs Johnstone that she will look after, giving him toys to play with and a bed of his own. She promises that in the end he 'could never be told / To stand and queue up / For hours on end at the dole' (38). She promises, too, more than material things; she will keep him warm in winter and cool in summer, always there if his dream is a nightmare. Whilst there is little real affection shown between her and Edward (and where there is, it is always too cloying and too needy), she does ensure he goes to a good school and has the chance to go to university. It is at the end of her song, when Mrs Johnstone sees the room Mrs Lyons is standing in, looking in *'awe at the comparative opulence and ease of the place'* but also when she hears Mrs Lyons' desperation, that Mrs Johnstone turns to her and agrees (37). From this perspective, it is possible to see a very different Mrs Lyons whose fear and obsession stems from a very real terror of losing her child. She believes what she is doing is 'for your own good. It's only because I love you Edward' (60). Even when she reaches for the knife to stab Mrs Johnstone it is not something she has thought about before but a last resort, an impulse as the stage directions tell us, when her attempt to payoff Mrs Johnstone again has failed. From this we can see a much more complex character emerge who moves beyond being a pantomime villain, telling a tragic story of love that goes wrong.

Linda

Linda first appears in the scene where the children are fighting battles and the first thing she does is to stand up to Sammy and defeat him, stopping his shots with a bin lid. At the end of the song, when the children, led by Sammy, are accusing Mickey of lying and saying he will fry in hell like a fish in a chip shop fat only five million times hotter, Linda '*moves in to protect*' him (64). She stands up to Sammy, undaunted, forcing him to beat a hasty withdrawal with his gang and then comforts Mickey, drying his tears and cheering him up. From this early scene, we learn two important things about Linda; she is brave and takes charge of things and she stands by Mickey, protecting him. In the early scenes, she is an equal to the boys, if not better. She hits the target when they go shooting (whereas both Edward and Mickey miss) and she joins in the joke about cheeking the policeman. Later in the play, we also see some more of her good-natured humour as she jokes with Edward: 'Well, hello sweetie pie; looking for a good time? Ten to seven (*She laughs*). Good time . . . ten to seven . . .' (106). As a young girl, she is very much one of the boys and one of the gang.

As they grow up and turn fourteen, she is still part of the gang, but inevitably relationships change. Sexual tensions start to emerge, at one point highlighted by Linda being caught in the centre of a game of piggy-in-the-middle played with a coconut. She still constantly sticks up for Mickey (when the bus conductor asks how old he is, it is Linda who answers for him and later when the teacher turns on him, she tells him to leave Mickey alone), showing her support for him but now she starts to talk about loving him, much to Mickey's embarrassment. She pursues her love over the next four years, declaring her love at every opportunity, even in front of 500 people in assembly. For one so proactive in so many other ways, she plays a very traditional role in not being able to initiate the relationship herself. In the end, it is Edward who finally makes Mickey ask her out.

From here, things move quickly. Linda gets pregnant and they marry but there is no fairy tale happy ever after. She becomes a housewife looking after her husband and child. Through everything that happens to Mickey, Linda is still strong and loyal. She visits him in prison, tries to persuade him to stop taking the drugs (she says she is depressed too but does not turn to pills to help) and, with Edward's help, sorts out a house and a job for him. She still needs and loves Mickey but when he will not stop taking the tablets, she gets frustrated. 'What about what I need?' she asks him. 'I need you. I love you. But, Mickey, not when you've got them inside you. When you take those things, Mickey, I can't even see you' (123). His answer is to take his work bag from her and grab his tablets.

In response she turns to Edward. She still has a glimmer inside her of the girl she used to be before she 'washed a million dishes' and it is in trying to get back some of who she used to be that she hesitantly goes to meet Edward (123). When they meet, they re-enact a moment from their childhood; Edward mimes firing a gun and it is in the laughter following this game that they kiss. He is the reminder of the 'half remembered song' of her childhood (123). Russell is at pains to point out that what happens between them is not meant to be cruel. They are 'two fools' who 'grasp at half a chance' (124). But as Mrs Johnstone sings 'Light Romance' to the same tune as 'Easy Terms', there is a clear feeling that a price will have to be paid, which is echoed in the image of Mickey hammering on the door 'calling for Linda, as he once did for his mother' (125). At the end, she can only run down the aisle, arriving as the twins lie dead, no longer able, as she was as a child, to protect Mickey.

Sammy

We hear about Sammy from Mickey before we see him. Firstly, Mickey wishes he was Sammy, despite the fact that he stole his toy car and broke it. Mickey sees his older brother as everything that is exciting, able to do daring things like drawing nudey women and weeing through the letter box. Secondly, Mickey tells Edward about Sammy. He hopes he is in a good mood because he can be 'dead mean sometimes' but even more excitingly, he has a plate in his head from where his sister, Donna Marie, dropped him out of the window (53). When he does appear, he leaps out in front of the twins, gun in hand, demanding a sweet. From here, Sammy is always associated with guns (and a catapult), the nature of the guns changing through the play from a toy to a real gun. It is this association and his role in the garage shooting, which can characterize Sammy as a 'bad boy'. He is also seen pulling a knife on the bus conductor and we hear that he has burned the school down when the family move. He is clearly a boy who is out of control and there is a fatalistic inevitability in his journey through the play, which leaves him in prison at the end.

Yet, Sammy is also a likeable character. As we have seen from Mickey's admiration of his older brother, there is more to him than guns and stealing and Mickey is not the only one to look up to him. He is the leader of the gang and the leader in the imaginative game played by the children, always raising the stakes from gun to bazooka to atom bomb. He may have killed the worms in his pocket (again) but he does want to give them a decent burial and seems genuinely perplexed that they keep dying. One of the things that engenders our sympathy is the fact that there seems to be no hope for him, no way that his life would (or could) have turned out differently, that he is let down by the world he finds himself in. The sympathy is created by these first scenes where we see a lively, charismatic boy who ends up on the dole at sixteen, with little hope. This is not presented as an excuse for his progression to armed robbery but the implied criticism seems to be of a world that does not make use of his energy and imagination and instead stifles it, as we see the teacher stifling Mickey in the school scene. Sammy is not simply aggressive he is also, in Linda's words, 'a soft get' (87).

Mr Lyons

Fathers are very absent in *Blood Brothers*, the twins' father appearing only briefly in the opening song. The strongest image of a father (and a husband) comes in Mr Lyons who appears after the birth of the twins, his absence working away from home allowing for Mrs Lyons' deception. When we first meet him, he appears proud of his wife and child and good natured but he is also rather distant. He is happy to leave his wife in charge of bringing up Edward and domestic arrangements, telling her 'you know best' (45). Although he shows concern about his wife's depression and acquiesces to her demands to move, he never really seems to understand or take her problems seriously, suggesting that she should see someone else (the doctor) to solve her problems. His main contribution to bringing up Edward is the provision of money, nice homes and an expensive education. Whilst he has one moment when he buys Edward a toy gun, spiritedly dying for him as they romp on the floor (an interesting moment to compare with Mickey 'shooting' his mother on page 49), he soon has to go, leaving Mrs Lyons to finish the story with their son.

Always in a hurry, constantly looking at his watch or impatiently blowing the car horn, his mind is elsewhere, needing to get to work. He tells his wife that when the merger is completed, 'the firm will run itself and I'll have plenty of time to spend with you both' (58). Instead, he all but disappears in Act Two. His final contribution is sacking Mickey, amongst others in his workforce who are 'surplus to requirement', reinforcing his indifference to the lives of people, and leaving the two mothers at the heart of the play (111). When the twins die, he and his wife are absent.

Things to do

- Write diaries for both Mickey and Edward, describing their first meeting. Think carefully about your written expression and make sure it is appropriate for each character. You could extend this by writing about other key moments in their relationship (for example about being in trouble with the policeman, moving to the country or their thoughts about Linda).

● Writing in the format of a play script, imagine the initial meeting between a director and an actor who has been cast in one of the main roles of *Blood Brothers*. Include the questions you think an actor might have and try to show the director's interpretation of the role through his/her answers.

Dramatic technique

When looking to describe a play, parallels with other works can help to understand what we are seeing. Care does need to be taken though and one of the temptations with *Blood Brothers* is to draw links with any other story that makes use of twins separated at birth. Most commonly, people look to Alexander Dumas' *The Corsican Brothers* (1844) but the story is very different (the twins in this story know they are twins and can feel each other's pain). Russell has said that although his story feels 'as if it's a story that has always existed', there is no existing story as far as he knows that parallels his one (Mulligan, 2005). But some comparisons do help locate the play in a wider framework and an understanding of these can help shed light on the play. Critics writing about *Blood Brothers* have chosen to describe it in a number of ways including:

Greek tragedy
Brechtian
Melodrama

Greek tragedy

The key ideas of Greek tragedy were laid out by Aristotle in the *Poetics* (335 BCE). These included:

- Tragedy depicts the downfall of a hero through a combination of hubris (human frailty or flaws) with the will of the gods.

- The hero has a flaw and/or makes a mistake (hamartia).

- There is a revelation (anagnorisis) or what Aristotle defined as 'a change from ignorance to awareness' (Aristotle, 1998, 15).

- Tragedy has the most effect on an audience when it is one family member who harms another.

The freelance director and former head of New Writing at the National Theatre, John Burgess, suggests tragedy is something which looks at the relationship between:

- Man and his own death and other men

- Man and gods and things that don't change

- Man and passions that live inside him.

BURGESS, 2005, xiii

It is possible to see some of these ideas at work in *Blood Brothers*. Mrs Johnstone's downfall, her path from happiness to misery, is the result of an error, i.e. giving away one of the twins. This is combined with her belief in superstition, which can be seen as a version of the gods. At the end, Mickey finds out the truth. There is a revelation, a change from ignorance of who Edward is to awareness that he is his twin and a realization he could have been him. The impact of Mrs Johnstone losing two of her children heightens our emotional response to the play because they are family. Connections to Greek tragedy can also be seen through the use of the narrator as a chorus (see 'Character' section) and another reason critics see echoes of Greek tragedy in the play is through Willy Russell's use of superstition or myths, in particular Mrs Lyons' story which feels like it should be an age-old tale.

Fate (or the will of the gods) which was also important in Greek tragedy is a difficult idea in the twenty-first century. We like to think that as individuals we are in control of our own destiny and the idea of things being predetermined can feel alien. Another way of thinking about fate might help think about how things work out in *Blood Brothers*. The characters are responsible for actions (i.e. they make choices) but there are forces outside of them (class and society) that are bigger than they are and mean they are not totally in control. For example, Mickey's decision to go on a job with Sammy comes about because he has lost his job through no fault of his own.

One reason it could be argued that *Blood Brothers* is not like a Greek tragedy is that Aristotle also said that tragedy should deal with characters of a 'high degree and reputation' (i.e. kings or noblemen) and the characters in *Blood Brothers* are ordinary people (Aristotle, 1998, 17). However, the American playwright Arthur Miller (1915–2005), in an essay called 'Tragedy and the Common Man' written in 1949, argued that 'the common man is as apt a subject for tragedy in its highest sense as kings were' and that 'insistence upon the rank of the tragic hero [. . .] is really but a clinging to the outward forms of tragedy' (Miller, 1977, 3; 5). In reviewing the play Logan argues *Blood Brothers* does attain Greek proportions 'while mocking the old argument – substantiated with reference to the Greeks – that low-status characters can't be tragic. Mickey Johnstone's class is his tragedy' (1998).

Brecht and epic theatre

Brecht was critical of naturalistic or, what he called, dramatic theatre. He believed that in this kind of theatre, the audience forgets their own lives and escapes into the lives of others, losing their ability to think. They hung 'up their brains with their hats in the cloakroom' and it 'drugged' the audience, rather like the tablets stop Mickey thinking (Brecht, 1986, 27). In its place he wanted a theatre that made his audience think, which he called epic theatre, and in order to prevent the audience from becoming too involved he reminded them throughout that they were watching a representation of life, not real life itself. He called the act of distancing the audience from emotional involvement (or empathy) the *verfremdungseffekt* (sometimes called the alienation effect but maybe better translated as making the familiar strange). To achieve this he used a number of theatrical devices and some of these can be seen in *Blood Brothers,* especially in the use of the narrator. For Brecht, epic theatre 'began to tell a story' from which the narrator was no longer missing and narration is used to remind the audience that they are watching the presentation of that story (Brecht, 1986, 71). Sometimes the narrator will tell the audience what happens before an audience sees it, which can help to ensure that they are less emotionally involved in the action as the outcome is already known (think about reading a story for the second time). *Blood Brothers* uses both a narrator and tells us at the start what will happen, so we become more interested in *how* it happens rather than *what* happens.

The narrator also speaks directly to the audience, breaking the fourth wall. In naturalistic theatre, the actor behaves as if they were the character and the audience was not present, adding to the illusion that this is reality. When the narrator asks us to judge how Mrs Johnstone has become a mother so cruel, he is not only asking us to think and make our minds up about something, he is also reminding us that we are watching a story. The narrator plays a number of different parts and at one moment the play even draws attention to this as Mrs Johnstone asks the narrator who appears as the gynaecologist (having just previously played the milkman), what he is doing there because the milk bill is not due until Thursday. Some of the cast also play multiple roles from children to people in the dole queue. For an audience, seeing the same actor play a number of roles reminds them that they are watching an actor, to use Brecht's word, demonstrating a character.

Brecht wanted sets that would suggest the world rather than represent it, 'a place need only have the credibility of a place glimpsed in a dream' (Brecht, 1986, 23). *Blood Brothers* moves through a number of locations, so the set can only be suggestive of places and sometimes characters move to new places very quickly (see 'Set' section). Brecht also used music to break up the action and comment on scenes, drawing attention to the theatricality by having the orchestra on the stage (as it was in the first production of *Blood Brothers*) and using different lighting for the songs. *Blood Brothers* does not use music to comment in the same way as Brecht, but the songs still remind us that this is theatre in the same way as some people say they do not like musicals because it is not realistic when people suddenly burst into song walking down the street.

One thing could be held up to say that *Blood Brothers* does not conform to Brechtian ideas of theatre – the emotional impact or connection we may feel to the story and the characters. Many people think Brecht wanted the audience to feel no emotion or empathy with what was happening on stage. In fact, what Brecht was wary of was the audience having similar emotions to the characters, believing this reinforced our conviction that these feelings were normal. Brecht said that 'when something seems "the most obvious thing in the world" it means that any attempt to understand the world has been given up' (Brecht, 1986, 71). Instead, he wanted the audience to ask if these experiences were indeed normal and if so whether they should be. He certainly was not against emotion saying that it simply was not true that epic theatre 'proclaims the slogan: "Reason this side, Emotion (feeling) that." It by no means renounces emotion' (Brecht, 1986, 227). So, if you find yourself reaching for the tissues as you leave the theatre as well as asking how a tragedy like *Blood Brothers* can happen, then you could argue you have just seen a piece of Brechtian theatre.

Melodrama

The word melodrama today tends to be used as a dismissive term for work that is heightened and simplistic and many of the critics that refer to *Blood Brothers* as a melodrama use it as a term of criticism. Brian Logan, for example, suggests the play is 'melodramatic' and 'over-insistent', criticising its simplicity (1998).

Melodrama was a popular nineteenth-century theatrical form associated with sensational events, exaggerated emotions and a simplified moral universe, where good was always good and bad was always bad. It included the use of music (*melos* means song or melody), often to signify character, and used stereotypical or stock characters. The heroine was always beautiful, morally upright and underwent a series of trials at the hands of the villain from which she was rescued by the handsome hero (usually with the help of his friend because the hero was not always very bright). They ended happily with the villain punished, or dead, and the couple united. From this description, it can be seen that *Blood Brothers* is very different to a melodrama with more complexity of character and plot (as well as not having a happy ending), although it is possible to see some connections. Some critics argue that aspects of the play are over-simplified. Brian Logan continues by saying the 'dice [. . .] are loaded against the well-to-do [the Lyons], and our sympathies are frog-marched towards the underdog [the Johnstones]', arguing that the parts for the Lyons 'are unsympathetically written' (Logan, 1998). The heightened emotions, especially in the final song, and what could be argued is a simplified argument about class could help to see *Blood Brothers* as having melodramatic aspects which, in contrast to the Brechtian aspects of the play, overwhelm our senses and by-pass our critical facilities.

Music and song

In a musical, songs do not exist to entertain, like a pop song. They are there to communicate the drama and musicals contain different kinds of songs to do different things. Some carry the plot forward, filling in gaps in the story (often known as narrative or action songs), some develop character, some reflect on themes. Songs also highlight emotion and evoke atmosphere and mood and they also serve to extend a moment. Saying 'I love you' takes a few seconds but Edward singing 'I'm Not Saying a Word' expands and repeats the idea giving it greater resonance. Many of the songs in the show are repeated also helping to create a sense of unity.

Narrative songs

The main narrative song is 'Marilyn Monroe', although it also serves thematically to create the connections between the film star and the characters of Mrs Johnstone and Mickey and in this sense also serves as a character song. It appears three times in the show, at the start of Act One and Act Two and it reappears when Mickey is in prison. Some narrative is also borne by the narrator's songs and 'One Summer' condenses four years into three pages.

Character songs

The twins share two songs, 'Lonely Sunday Afternoon/My Friend' and 'That Guy' which, whilst singing about their differences, establishes the connections between them. There is a lot to be learned about Mrs Lyons from her duet with Mrs Johnstone and whilst Mrs Johnstone's theme is about making a decision, Mrs Lyons' section of the song reveals her loneliness and her desire for a child of her own. All three songs are duets, bringing together characters who are separated in the play, finding some harmony between them.

Mrs Johnstone has two songs that reveal her character. 'Bright New Day', the most upbeat song in the show, reflects her optimistic nature and her dreams of escaping. 'Tell Me It's Not True' underlines her inability to accept what has happened and her desperation at the death of the twins. As the final song in the play, it also provides the emotional climax to the story, starting with the plaintive, imploring voice of Mrs Johnstone singing alone and building into a finale sung by the whole company, growing in volume and power.

Edward's love song is also a character song, showing that like Mickey, he is unable to *talk* about his feelings but he can *sing* about them and even then he keeps saying that is not really what he is saying. 'If I was him,' he insists, 'I'd bring you flowers/and ask you to dance.' But because he is not him, he 'is not saying a word' (108). This kind of song is known as a conditional love song in musicals. As with the two duets, it also shows Edward wishing he could be in Mickey's shoes and the simplicity of the tune reflects Edward's immature character.

Thematic songs

The song which carries the most thematic resonance is 'Easy Terms'. At the start, it appears to be a straightforward song about Mrs Johnstone's things being repossessed. They have only been hers on borrowed time. But as she stands there with the twins in the pram, it becomes a song about losing one of them. 'Easy terms' might be a phrase associated with paying for something in instalments (as is the never never, when something is never paid for) but it is also a term for being close to someone. As she moves through the song, the focus changes and the third verse is clearly about losing one of the babies. This sense of loss is emphasized when a verse of the song recurs later in the play as Mrs Johnstone sends Edward away. The song also highlights the themes of the price to be paid and fear about who might be at the door and when the tune reappears as 'Light Romance', it alerts the audience to the fact that there will be a price to be paid for Linda and Edward's actions.

Mood songs

The show starts with an overture, a melancholic, hymn like vocal with no words out of which comes the yearning voice of Mrs Johnstone singing 'Tell me it's not true/Say it's just story' (29). This sets the mood before a word has been spoken. Much of the mood after this is created by the narrator's song which reappears several times with its driving rhythm suggesting nothing will be able to stop it, just as no-one will be able to stop the inevitable ending, adding a seam of tension and menace. One musical influence on Willy Russell is traditional ballads, in particular the Child Ballads, a collection of fifteenth- and sixteenth-century songs made by Francis Child. Despite their name, they are not children's songs but often dark stories of murder or the supernatural (not the slow and romantic songs we tend to associate with the term today) and the narrator's song is a good example of this influence and, in fact, the whole show has the structure and feel of a ballad.

Music in the play also serves to underscore moments creating mood. Irving Wardle suggests the most 'telling moments are sustained beds of sound underlying the dialogue' projecting the desolation of a lonely Sunday or the dark-side of children's games' (1983). Sound effects (usually played by the band) also help underline moments. Not many are indicated in the text suggesting the importance of those that are specified. At the moment Mrs Johnstone lays her hand on the Bible to swear she will not tell anyone the truth, there is 'a bass note, repeated as a heartbeat' (39). This runs through the ensuing scene, growing in intensity, as the narrator reminds the audience that 'the pact is sealed' and 'a deal has been done'. It reaches its climax as he ends on a 'debt is a debt and must be paid' underlining the importance of the section, but it is then replaced by the sound of crying babies helping to reinforce tension but also reminding us of the impending birth of the babies and the moment when the promise will have to be kept (40).

Two songs are harder to categorize. 'The Kids Song' sets up a world of children playing on the streets, introducing guns and killing. Musically, it sounds as though it could be being played on the street by banging bin lids together, as the percussion underscores a world of imaginative games. It is the kind of song in musicals often called 'the ordinary world' song serving to create the everyday life that the play is set in. The Lyons' world, in contrast, does not have its own song. The other song that is hard to categorize is 'Take a Letter Mrs Jones'. It is the song that is most about the context of the show, reflecting on the impact of unemployment and musically it has echoes of 2Tone, a musical form popular in the early eighties with its use of brass instruments. It also moves the story along by showing the wedding and Mickey losing his job, and being sung by Mr Lyons it tells something about his character. His clipped vocal style and refined accent create a sense of not caring about the impact of what he is doing (dictating redundancy letters) and combined with the lyrics which are emotionless (it is just another sign of the times, he tells Mrs Jones before he sacks her too) create an image of an unfeeling man while we watch the human impact of his actions as the dole queue lengthens.

To understand how the music works in the play, you need to listen to the songs. All the text gives you are the lyrics but the real meaning is made not just by the words on the page. The style of the music and how the singer/actor delivers the song, also add to the meaning. Writing about music is difficult but you do not need to have a very detailed knowledge of music to see some of the implications in performance. For example, compare the versions of 'Marilyn Monroe' from Barbara Dickson's original recording with Kiki Dee's version. The former starts with a cheerful introduction and is more upbeat, only slowing down when she sings about looking forty-two, giving a sense of someone living through a good time when she was young. The version by Kiki Dee is much slower and more wistful, as if she is looking back on being young and happy rather than living it.

Set

At the start of the play, the production note offers some advice on the setting saying 'the whole play should flow along easily and smoothly with no cumbersome scene changes'. The only semi-permanent areas are the Lyons' comfortable home and the exterior front door of the Johnstone's house. The area between the two houses acts as 'communal ground' for street scenes. Apart from this note there is little description of the set in the play although it contains a large number of different settings including:

- The Lyons' lounge
- The Johnstone's terraced house
- Their new houses in the country (including Mrs Johnstone's kitchen)
- The street
- The gynaecologist's office
- The park
- The Lyons' garden
- The bus stop and the bus
- Two schools
- The hill above the estate
- The street outside the cinema
- The funfair
- Prison
- Mickey and Linda's house
- The Town Hall

The action moves very quickly between these different places (for example, it goes from Mickey's school to Mrs Lyons' house to the hill above the estate in three pages) and a simple staging means the play can keep moving without pauses or blackouts, allowing for a sense of continuity in the story and giving a sense of relentlessly moving forwards towards the conclusion.

Sometimes the text itself helps us to understand where we are. When Mickey asks Edward to come to the park he is in the garden. We recognize this when Mickey encourages him to 'bunk under y'fence' (67). We realize Mickey and Linda are climbing a hill outside the estate because Linda complains about her high heels sinking into the ground and having to walk over a load of fields and we know they are on a hill when Mickey says 'y'can see the estate from up here' (93). But, given the lack of precise set description in the text, much of the set we associate with the play has come from decisions that designers have made based on the production notes and the demands of the script. The 'semi-permanent' setting used for many productions depicts the Lyons' lounge on one side of the stage using some of the clues in the text about what needs to be in this room (a table where the shoes get put, a shelf of books where the dictionary is kept) alongside indications of the Lyons' class. This contrasts with the opposite side of the stage where a line of terraced houses with peeling paint, fading graffiti and milk bottles on the step includes Mrs Johnstone's front door. These houses are not complete facades but stop halfway up helping to keep in mind that this is not real. Its proximity to the Lyons' house, of which we see only one room suggesting a much bigger house, maintains the contrast of the two lives throughout the play. At the back a grey skyline of Liverpool dominates Act One (changing to the countryside in Act Two), helping to locate the play in the city. Sometimes small pieces of set are used to suggest a location. The bus is a line of scruffy bench seats and a steering wheel. The school is a few desks and the funfair is flashing neon signs with the shapes of rides appearing above the houses. At other times, the set is flown in to define a space for the prison or the Town Hall. All of this is suggestive of a world rather than a realistic representation.

The non-naturalistic set not only maintains the theatricality of the play but also allows for non-naturalistic (or over-lapping) staging. At times, characters appear on stage when they are not part of the scene and this can add to their character. For example, Edward watches unnoticed as the children play, supposedly in his garden, suggesting his loneliness and later, when he has moved to the country and Mickey is bored and lonely, he appears in his own garden *'equally bored and alone'* suggesting a connection between the twins (77). The stage directions tell us this might just be in Mickey's imagination. The space occupied by Eddie and Mickey most of the time is the space between the houses, an empty space, emphasizing the way they are caught between two worlds and trying to find a way of meeting on neutral ground. So, the set can operate in a way that is not always literal but helps develop the sub text.

Costume

As with the set, there is little indication in the text for costume but in the production it works to help establish class and also the time period. For example, Sammy as a sixteen-year-old appears in a black leather jacket with 'Status Quo' (a rock band that were popular in the 1970s) on the back, with the jacket also indicating that he is a bit of a tearaway. A comparison of Mrs Johnstone's and Mrs Lyons' costumes helps to show how costume indicates class. Apart from a brief glimpse of Mrs Johnstone at the start as a carefree young girl in a fifties-style dress and looking a little like Marilyn Monroe, she wears wraparound sleeveless aprons to cover her slightly dowdy catalogue clothing. This suggests someone who is always working, either at her cleaning job or as a mother looking after her children. In contrast, Mrs Lyons is immaculately dressed, with jewelry and high heels. When she first appears she has been shopping and she appears in a variety of different costumes throughout, suggesting she has a large wardrobe.

The twins' costumes also show the class differences between them. Mickey at seven is ragged and dirty, with tousled hair, falling down socks and a too big hand-me-down jumper which is out of shape, often pulled down over his knees or over his head. As he grows up, his shorts are swapped for jeans and a school blazer with a carelessly knotted tie. Later the blazer is replaced with a parka and then a donkey jacket symbolizing someone who is a manual worker. Edward is always neat, tidy and well ironed with well-cut and shining hair. The grey shorts and tidily pulled up socks he wears at seven become firstly grey flannel trousers (matched with a smart public school blazer), later corduroys (paired with a duffel coat and college scarf) and eventually a suit as he mirrors the costume Mr Lyons wears.

Language

Like his home city which is renowned for the pleasure it takes in language and story-telling, Willy Russell likes 'to revel in the language' and the play makes use of the words, phrases and accents of Liverpool (Gill, 1992, 1–2). It is the Johnstone family who speak with the broadest accents and use the most colloquial language. People are dead mean, dead careful, dead funny or dead worried, where dead means very, rather than deceased. People are referred to as 'Our Sammy' or 'me husband', greeted by Hi-yas and waved off with Ta-ras. All of these phrases bring a flavour of the language of the city to the stage. 'All youse lot swear', Linda says to the gang and swear words also pepper the Johnstone children's language (64). Edward's delight at learning to swear is one of the things that brings the twins together. However, he never sounds quite right when he swears making Mickey laugh because 'it sounds dead funny swearin' in that posh voice' (95). When Edward tells his mother she is 'a fuckoff', his misuse of the word adds to the sense that it is not his natural idiom (60).

Instead of swearing or using colloquialisms, Edward uses words like 'super fun' and 'smashing' and, like his parents, does not have a Liverpool accent. A strong Liverpool accent here is used to denote class, a point also made by the use of the twins' names. No one calls Mickey, Michael and it is Mickey who calls Edward, Eddie. The Lyons' refer to their son by his full name and use formal language and old fashioned phrases, Mr Lyons referring to his son as 'old chap' (72). The differences can also be seen in the words the boys use for their mothers. To Mickey, Mrs Johnstone is usually 'Mam' (a term common in Liverpool) and occasionally 'Mother'. Edward uses 'Mummy' and occasionally 'My Ma'. The first meeting of the twins is also a good illustration of the differences in the use and understanding of language. Mickey whispers 'the 'F' word' in Edward's ear. Then Edward turns to him to ask what it means.

> **Mickey** I don't know. It sounds good though doesn't it?
> **Edward** Fantastic. When I get home I'll look it up in the dictionary.
> **Mickey** In the what?
> **Edward** The dictionary. Don't you know what a dictionary is?
> **Mickey** 'Course I do . . . It's a, it's a thingy innit?
> **Edward** A book which explains the meaning of words.
> **Mickey** The meaning of words, yeh. (53)

Edward's instinct is to find out the meaning of words in a book. Mickey is not convinced by Edward's explanation of what a dictionary is and revels more in his pleasure at the sound of the language. He likes words because they sound good.

Language also helps to define characters and highlight themes. Mrs Lyons' language changes through the play from being confident and authoritarian to desperate and emotive as she descends into madness, using language which makes the listener feel more intensely (as opposed to emotional language which is characterized by intense feeling in the way that it is said). The narrator's language is poetic and old-fashioned, at times emphasizing the timelessness of the story and suggesting its locations in the past and in myth, making him seem less realistic and emphasizing his authority and wisdom. The play also uses a lot of repetition. Phrases like 'the devil's got your number' and 'a debt is a debt that must be paid' act like a chorus, add to the lyrical feeling and also help create unity in a play that sprawls over decades.

Things to do

- Design a set for the play, taking in to account all the locations it needs to include and any information you can glean from the play about what it needs to contain.

- In pairs, make a list of all the songs in the play. Once your list is complete, for each song decide on three or four words that you feel best describe its mood and impact on the audience.

- Compare Kiki Dee's and Barbara Dickson's versions of 'Tell Me It's Not True' (available online). Which version do you prefer and why?

- Create some short scenes between Mickey/Edward or Mrs Johnstone/Mrs Lyons (for example, you could decide to recreate Mrs Johnstone's interview for her job or Mickey and Edward meeting up again in the school holidays). Think carefully about the different kinds of language they use. Consider, for example, how they say hello and goodbye, what they call each other and their accents.

Critical reception

Willy Russell has said: 'If you have got a play that lasts as long as *Blood Brothers* does it is amazing looking at the historical shift in the way it is viewed. Initially some of the hostility towards it was vitriolic.' Some reviewers have seen the show more than once and have changed their minds about the play in the process. Here, the novelist Beryl Bainbridge (1932–2010) comments on seeing the show for a second time in 2002.

I first went to see the shows eight years ago, and failed to appreciate it. I think I was still thinking of musicals in terms of *Guys and Dolls* and *Oklahoma!*, whose songs were more memorable than the storyline. Seeing *Blood Brothers* for the second time recently, I now realize that I ought to have thought of the music as a moving accompaniment to a very dark and affecting drama. (197, 2002)

Writing in 1983, Steve Grant suggests some of the reasons for the differing opinions which might be useful in thinking about why critics have responded in different ways.

Of all the types of contemporary theatre on offer, surely the musical exerts the greatest amount of controversy. Add to this the North v South element which runs through all such cultural exchanges and you have a potential minefield of opposing viewpoints. London critics and theatregoers are apt to find provincial shows unsophisticated and politically naïve. Supporters will reply that the North has put the working classes back into the theatre, is more exuberant and down to earth than its more rarified and modish Southern counterpart.

Things to do

Read through the following review extracts, all taken from the tenth anniversary of *Blood Brothers* in the West End, picking out any words, phrases and ideas that are used to praise or criticise the play. Look up any unfamiliar words in a dictionary.

'Willy Russell's *Blood Brothers* has been trundling along in the West End for 10 years now – more if you include the original, unsuccessful production – and I must say I've never paid it much heed [. . .] *Blood Brothers* is melodramatic, of course, and over-insistent. The Narrator – who is Russell's Greek chorus – disseminates doom-laden ditties between every single scene; his over-earnest fatalism casts too dark a shadow. Similarly, Russell [. . .] can't resist contrasting the twins' parallel experiences. When the nippers are nicked for stone-throwing, the local bobby shares a drink with Mr Lyons, but only sharp words with Mrs Johnstone. Elsewhere, infant Mickey rides his imaginary horse like John Wayne. Edward as if he's at his first gymkhana. And Edward's first term at the university is thrown into grim relief by Mickey's grinding experience of the dole. The dice, in other words, are loaded against the well-to-do, and our sympathies are frog-marched towards the underdog. It's no coincidence that the productions weaker performances are the wealthier family; the parts are unsympathetically written.' (Brian Logan)

'Next to this tremendously satisfying, passionately felt show, the recent flurry of new musicals (*Dr Dolittle*, *Whistle Down the Wind*) seems all the more plastic, pointless and bloodless. *Blood Brothers* is a gripping, gritty – and superbly hummable – drama [. . .] Russell's angry social document is cunningly disguised as melodrama. And with the savage inexorability of Greek tragedy, the truth burns its way out. [. . .] While tears are guaranteed, so is laughter . . .' (Georgina Brown)

'Its roots are deep in the myth about twins separated at birth, the one that always served the Greeks and Shakespeare well enough; and although it is unmistakeably set in the Liverpool of the early 1980s, *Blood Brothers* remains almost alarmingly topical since none of its central issues of poverty, unemployment and class warfare has gone away in the meantime.' (Sheridan Morley)

'For those who haven't seen it – as I hadn't until last week – it's the story of a Liverpudlian working-class mother, desperately short of funds [. . .] A show that runs for 10 years without benefit of hype or lavish effects is plainly giving people something they want. On the night I was there the audience rose to its feet at the end, as I am told it usually does, with near-religious rapture. [. . .] my own feelings are mixed. The show *does* have an undeniable driving force, but its folk-tale elements are jumbled up with a good deal that is downright corny, some of its social judgements have the crudeness of a badly drawn cartoon, and matters aren't helped by the presence of a lugubrious narrator . . .' (John Gross)

'How to explain the durability of Willy Russell's *Blood Brothers*, which celebrates, in my view deservedly, its tenth birthday in the West End this week? [. . .] *Blood Brothers* would scarcely have run for a decade if it were at root an earnest treatise about the inequality of opportunity in modern England. Whatever its rational pretensions, the piece beats with a primitive heart. Russell virtually concedes as much by failing to explain why, in defiance of social probability and the class logic he is busily exposing, Eddie and Mickey meet as boys, exchange blood vows, and remain close friends into their prime. He is exploiting the myths and legends about the eerie symbiosis of twins. He is writing a folk ballad for the Thatcher and post-Thatcher eras – and why not?' (Benedict Nightingale)

'Adroitly entwining the culturally specific and the mythic, the show expresses pain at the human devastation caused by Thatcherite economics via a folk-tale plot [. . .] Threaded through the saltily amusing script and the open-hearted score are familiar Russell themes: the gains and losses of upward mobility; the difficulty of assessing the advantages in another person's social situation from a non-self-referring perspective (*cf* the hairdresser and the don in *Educating Rita*); the burdens of being a woman and the yearning to escape from domestic drudgery [. . .] its heart is in the right place – how many musicals present a social argument of any kind? For that alone I raise my glass.' (Paul Taylor)

Some things you might want to consider having read these extracts are:

- Why some of the critics admit they have not been to see the show even though it has been running for ten years.

- How some of the writers reveal their attitude to the audience and to the popularity of the show through their use of language.

- How some critics are wary of, and sometimes dismissive of, emotion.

- How some writers discuss why the show had lasted so long in the West End and the kinds of other work they relate it to.

Things to do

Write a response to one of the review extracts above, putting forward your own perspective on the play.

Related work

Willy Russell's plays

Many of Willy Russell's plays share themes in common with *Blood Brothers,* themes of trying (and failing) to escape, education, the impact of class and the hope that life could be better. *Educating Rita* (1980), in contrast to *Blood Brothers*, offers the possibility of choice. Rita comes late to education, breezing into Frank's university office declaring she wants to know everything. Frank becomes increasingly concerned that the kind of education he can offer which will teach her to quote literary critics and pass exams will take away what is unique about Rita. Towards the end, when she understands the rules and rituals of education, he asks if this is all she wanted, if she has 'come all this way for so very, very little?' (Russell, 1996, 355). But for Rita what is important is that education has given her a choice where none previously existed. Unlike the twins in *Blood Brothers* who have no choices but are bound by fate, Rita can make her own decisions and for her that ability is life itself. *Our Day Out* (made for television 1977; staged 1983), a play with songs, also offers some useful points of connection and contrast with *Blood Brothers*. Alongside arguments about other possible ways of lives being lived, it includes a debate about what education is about for working-class children with Mrs Kay (who has organized the outing to Wales) determined that the children will at the very least have a good day out. 'It's too late for them', she tells another teacher, Mr Briggs, because nobody knows what to do with them (Russell, 1996, 148).

Jim Cartwright's *Road* (1986)

Like *Blood Brothers*, *Road* 'has come to represent a period of British social history which saw the marked polarisation of the classes and an exacerbation of the north–south divide' (Milling, 2012, 247). It too explores the impact of Thatcherism and offers an alternative representation of the north from that seen in soap operas like *Coronation Street* (set in Manchester) or *Brookside* (set in Liverpool and running from 1982 to 2003). *Road* takes place somewhere on the very edge of a town somewhere in Lancashire, although Cartwright says 'it might be in Liverpool or Bolton or Middlesbrough or Newcastle' (Cartwright quoted in Milling, 2012, 225). It too has a narrator who guides the audience on a journey over one day, meeting the inhabitants of the road as they drink, fight, try to have a good time and pine for the past. The play was performed as a promenade show where the theatre seats are removed, taking the actors closer to the audience than Russell does.

Funny and tragic like *Blood Brothers*, *Road* suggests there are not always solutions to the problems of unemployment and lack of hope. Joey takes to his bed to starve because there is nothing else left to do. He is after something that is missing because 'life can't be just this, can it? What everybody's doing.' (Cartwright, 1996, 40). As he lies there, he tries to make sense of the world in a long monologue that has the same hurt and anger heard from Mickey at the end of *Blood Brothers*.

> I'm sick of people, people, stupid people. Frying the air with their mucky words, their mucky thoughts, their mucky deeds [. . .] Where has man gone? Why is he so wrong? Why am I hurt all the way through? Every piece of me is bruised or gnawed raw [. . .] What did I do? What was my crime? Who do I blame?!
>
> CARTWRIGHT, 1996, 42–3

He demands to know who has done this to him and why, blaming business and religion for murdering the child in the man. Although as he dies he concludes there are no solutions, the play ends with an attempt to grasp at possibilities. As four of the characters drink wine and listen to Otis Redding's 'Try a Little Tenderness', which reminds them of feelings you keep forgetting, they start to demand magic and miracles and 'light out on the pavement', as they desperately cling together chanting, 'somehow, a somehow, might escape' (Cartwright, 1996, 83).

Lee Hall's *Billy Elliot: The Musical* (based on the film made in 2000; music by Elton John, 2005)

A number of musicals can be seen to provide influences for *Blood Brothers*, including Lionel Bart's *Oliver!* (1960). Like *Blood Brothers*, it is definably British (it takes the audience on a journey through Dickensian London) but still achieved international success. More recently, Lee Hall's *Billy Elliot*, notably the stage musical rather than the film, offers parallels. It too is set in the north (this time in the north-east) and makes use of the language of the region (the programme provides translations for some of the show's language). It too is about how the world you are born into can shape and restrict your life and it too uses dancing as a means of escape and self-expression, but here Billy, the son of a miner, overcomes family bigotry and financial hardship to escape to the Royal Ballet School. His success is set against the background of the 1984–5 miners' strike and his personal triumph is counter-pointed with the community's decline, the show ending with the collapse of the strike. Unlike *Blood Brothers*, this is a very male world, full of muscular choreography as miners come up against the police. Billy's mother has died two years before and whilst she is a ghostly presence in the show, it is Billy's relationship with his father and brother that form the centre of the work. It also offers a more politicized criticism of Thatcherism, starting with grainy film celebrating the nationalization of the coal industry in 1945 and including a song that celebrates the fact that Margaret Thatcher is one day closer to her death. Lee Hall, in the programme, sees the play as showing 'that we are all capable of making lives for ourselves which are full of joy and self-expression' whatever our circumstances. This stands in stark contrast to Mickey's story.

Alan Bleasdale's *Boys from the Blackstuff* (1982)

Although a television series, *Boys from the Blackstuff* is an important work in relation to *Blood Brothers*. It has come to speak for a nation under Thatcher. It added two catch phrases, 'gizza a job' and 'I can do that', to the national vocabulary. creating a folk hero for the 1980s in the shape of Yosser Hughes. Written by fellow Liverpuddlian, Alan Bleasdale, and set in Liverpool it focuses on five men who have lost their jobs and are working on the side whilst signing on. Yosser's story is the most often cited following him as he loses his job, his wife, his children, his house and his self-respect. He is reduced to head-butting lamp-posts, lift walls, confessional boxes, and policemen in an attempt to articulate his despair and take away the pain. As an image of the impact of unemployment, the series gives an insight into the cost to people's lives and the city of Liverpool in the 1980s.

Glossary of dramatic terms

Breaking the fourth wall   The fourth wall is the imaginary wall that exists between actors on the stage and the audience. No such wall actually exists but the term means that actors pretend they cannot see or hear the audience. Breaking the fourth wall means the actors acknowledge the audience and may talk directly to them (as the narrator does in *Blood Brothers*).

Catharsis   A term used by Aristotle in *Poetics* which means the relieving of emotional tensions (or excesses) through watching tragedy. He does not discuss the term in detail and there is a lot of argument about quite what he meant by it. One way to think about it is the way you feel better after watching a sad film that has made you cry.

Dramatic irony   This is a device by which a playwright draws on knowledge that the audience have, but the characters in the play do not, in order to create dramatic tension. The fact that the audience knows the truth about the twins whilst the boys do not means that *Blood Brothers* is constructed around dramatic irony. Other moments also contain dramatic irony, for example, when Edward asks Mrs Lyons if she has a secret too.

Episodic   This kind of dramatic structure is associated with the plays of Brecht and involves lots of relatively short scenes linked together by the same character, place or theme. In Brecht, scenes could be moved around and placed in a different order because there is no overall beginning, middle and end. In *Blood Brothers*, scenes unfold in a chronological way but there are jumps of time.

Foreshadowing   This is when a writer hints at a theme or circumstance early on in their play that will later be developed more explicitly. In *Blood Brothers*, for example, the children's game and Edward giving Mickey the present of a gun foreshadow the ending.

Motif   A recurring idea or object in a text that has a symbolic significance. Through its repetition, it can help highlight important ideas and themes.

Naturalism   Naturalism is a style of theatre, usually connected to the work of theatre practitioner Constantin Stanislavski and late nineteenth/early twentieth-century playwrights such as Anton Chekhov and Henrik Ibsen. It involves the detailed and realistic representation of life on stage.

Open stage   Traditional proscenium arch stages (which look like a box with a picture frame on the side open to the audience) keep the audience and the actors separate and lend themselves to illusionistic theatre. Open stages, which can take on a variety of physical configurations, allow for much closer actor/audience relationship. The original version of *Blood Brothers* for schools was in the round with the audience sitting on all four sides of the stage.

Prologue   A separate introductory section of a work. It establishes the setting and gives background information. It comes from the Greek words *pro* (before) and *logos* (the world). It can be a separate speech, as Russell refers to when he talks about *Henry V*, or a scene (and a song) as in *Blood Brothers*.

Set   The set is the environment that is constructed on a stage for a play to take place within. For more detail on this, see the section on 'Design' within 'Dramatic technique'.

Setting   The setting is the place or places in which the fictional world of the play occurs, which may be represented by the set. Whilst the set is a real space, inhabited by actors, the setting is a fictional space, inhabited by characters.

Soliloquy   The act of speaking one's thoughts aloud when alone or regardless of anyone else who might seem to hear what you are saying. Mickey's rhyme about Sammy is one example in *Blood Brothers*. The twins' song, when they are both on stage together but cannot seem to hear what the other is saying, is another.

Subtext   There are two ways for dramatists to reveal information about their characters and narrative. They can state information directly and explicitly in the text. For example, a character can tell another character what they are thinking or feeling, or about something that has happened to them in the past. However, relying too much on this sort of dialogue can lead to clunky and awkward writing. Playwrights are aware that, in real life, people do not always immediately tell each other what is bothering them or how they are feeling. This has led dramatists to make frequent use of subtext, where a character's dialogue says one thing directly, but may imply or suggest other things, through what is left unsaid or by the way the actor is instructed to say the lines. In *Blood Brothers*, the narrator sometime functions to tell us what a character is feeling.

Unity of time and place   Derived from Aristotle's *Poetics*, these are plays in which the action is limited to a single plot (unity of action), a single location (unity of place), and the events of a single day (unity of time). *Blood Brothers*, spanning more than two decades and moving through a number of locations, does not conform to this model.

Well made play   This is a kind of play traditionally associated with late nineteenth-century theatre which followed a series of rules including a tight plot (often connected to a missing letter or information that has fallen into the wrong hands), a revelation and a denouement (an unfolding of the events at the end). It has come to be used for plays that follow a traditional structure observing unities of time and place. Examples can be seen in (some of) the work of Terence Rattigan, Ibsen and Alan Ayckbourn.

CHAPTER TWO

Behind the Scenes

Willy Russell (WR)

RM: Why do we start with the end?

WR: I learnt very early on the truth about tragedy. The catharsis that is achieved through tragedy is a cyclical thing. People do go to see *Hamlet* time and time again or they can go to see Arthur Miller's *Death of a Salesman* many, many times. And every time, subsequent to your first visit, you take your seat knowing the end. Now what does that do? Knowing the end, contrary to expectation, doesn't diminish the theatrical experience for you. It heightens it and makes matters more important because you are watching it knowing that this character and this situation are moving towards doom. Now, I'm not William Shakespeare or Arthur Miller. I can't give the audience the benefit of knowing the story and they might never come and see it again. Instead, I show them the end so they know that these twins are going to die and that heightens everything. In the same way, some narrative ballad singers would sing the end of the song first to let the audience know and then go back to the beginning of the song. And often again, people would listen to the same songs time and time and time again and it gets richer with the retelling.

RM: Why does that happen?

WR: Because we are human beings and your watching of the piece is now more loaded because you are not watching it to find out what happens. Of course, the need to know what happens next is primal but sometimes you need to work in a different way. Take *Tom and Jerry*. You watch *Tom and Jerry*, merely because you need to know what happens next, because you need to know if the cat gets the mouse. You *don't* watch it because of the flaw in the character of the cat that takes him inexorably towards his own doom. Now, when you see *Blood Brothers*, you see them playing a game in the first act and they are saying the whole thing is just a game. It's full of allusions to the doom it will eventually reach and you wouldn't see that if you didn't know what was going to happen. The fact that I use a lot of humour and comedy on the journey is because I don't want it to be a doom-laden evening. Tragedy should not have a feeling of hopelessness because, even though you know what will happen, you still sit there hoping that Hamlet will take some kind of action that will avoid that end.

RM: It is also very episodic structurally.

WR: I was introduced to that form of theatre really before I went to theatre because when I was twenty I went back to education, after having had such a spectacularly failed time at school, and I did 'O' Level (GCSE) English Literature. I was introduced to Shakespeare for the first time because, like a lot of people, I had a terrible prejudice against Shakespeare and we studied *Henry V*. One of the things I noticed early on was that a Shakespeare play was closer to a movie structure than it was to a play. I had seen plays on television which were well-made plays that observed unities of time and place, but Shakespeare didn't. You want a new scene, a character comes on, tells you where the scene is and you just move on effortlessly. He even says at the beginning of *Henry V*, audience help us with this will you. The chorus comes on at the start and says we're going to do incredible things during the next two hours. We're going to see massive armies of thousands of men. We're going to sail galleons across the Channel. We've got to go to France and all we've got is this little bit of wood called our stage. But, audience if you lend us your imaginations we'll get there, we'll see the battles and we'll be on the galleons.

Then, of course, I went to the Everyman Theatre where there was a similar style, which was *loose* and episodic, a sprawling house-style that had grown up through the efforts of John McGrath[1] and Alan Dossor.[2] Their influences had come through Brecht shot through with a fun-loving, anarchic Joan Littlewood[3] approach to theatre. They wanted theatre to matter to the mass of the people in whose city the theatre existed. So when I wrote my first big play for them, *John, Paul, George, Ringo and Bert*, I remember saying to Alan Dossor, because I had an idea of setting it in a room somewhere and observing the unities of time and space, do you want that or do you want me to write it in the Everyman house style with songs, a narrator moving in and out, comedy, addressing the audience and acknowledging that there is an audience that were in a theatre? And that is what he wanted. Interestingly, I saw him on the first night of *Blood Brothers* at the Lyric and he was full of praise and I said to him, 'You do realize it came out of the Everyman house style.'

I also did a piece in Edinburgh called *Sam O'Shanker* that had piano accompaniment and we'd borrowed and hired things like rain machines and thunder sheets and wind machines. In rehearsals, we were at the point where Sam O'Shanker was driving off and the rain was falling and I suddenly said to everyone, 'Do you know what, this is ridiculous. Let's just get two benches, bring it all out front, and

---

[1] John McGrath (1935–2002) was a writer and founder of the theatre company 7:84.

[2] Alan Dossor is a theatre director who was artistic director of Liverpool Everyman Theatre from 1970–1975.

[3] Joan Littlewood (1914–2002) was a theatre director who ran Theatre Royal Stratford East in London from 1953–1975.

put it on the stage.' So the audience could see somebody creating the wind. When we had a lightening flash, I got somebody to cut a big arrow out of card and you just threw the card across the stage. There were gales of laughter. You could see the piano being played but it still created a tension when you needed it. So when I got to *Blood Brothers* I am working with the director Chris Bond. Chris is a product of the Liverpool Everyman and all that kind of style so I don't even have to have a dialogue with him about this. The whole of the band will be on stage in a very prominent position, high up in the gantry, so that you, the audience, at any point can look and see a keyboard player, a flautist, a violinist. You can see them changing instruments, and turning over their score. When we get to a point in the play when we can use the band to drop in 'To Let' signs and 'For Sale' Signs and 'city in decay' signs, they join in. In the kid's game, they throw stuff down and shout. That's how *Blood Brothers* was originally conceived and produced. It is as open to the audience as is possible. Now, over the years it has been taken further back on to the stage. I'm not saying that is not a valid way to do it. You could make an argument that the production has been running for a long time and it is much more of a successful production than the Liverpool Playhouse production which only ran for six months in the West End. But, for me, that original production is my type of theatre.

RM: What aspects of the first production made it your kind of theatre?

WR: One interesting thing about the first production is that while I compose music I don't formally write notation, so I record it. I would do a demo with the musical director on this little studio set up, so when we got to do the show, all of the songs were written and demoed. We wanted to hire musicians in a different way to normal. Usually, in a musical, you just have a piano player in rehearsals who plays all the band parts, because bands are very expensive things. Then you move into the theatre and that's when your band comes in and because they are playing from scores and they are fast sight readers that is considered completely fine. We didn't want to go down that route. We wanted it to be much more of an organic process because we wanted the band to play with a certain feel that doesn't come easily if you are reading from a score. We didn't give the band carte blanche. Everything was written but it was given to them in demo form so they had to listen to it and play it rather than read it. Lots of bands work like that. John Lennon and Paul McCartney did exactly the same thing. They didn't write the stuff down. So it meant we had the band in rehearsal from day one and Chris could say, for example, there's a moment early on where Eddie gives Mickey the gift of a gun when he is leaving and Chris said wouldn't it be lovely to underscore that moment, get the trumpet player to play some bars of the chorus from 'Easy Terms' plaintively in the background. If you've got the traditional pit band, you can't do that kind of stuff because it's not written down. So it meant that we had that freedom to tap into the band whenever we wanted to.

It should also be said that the style was dictated by the first small version of the play for schools because we could only have five actors. So I had to come up with the idea of the narrator who played every other small role that was required and in the original full production at Liverpool Playhouse that is exactly what we did. It's about moving fast and it's about saying to the audience, one minute he's the narrator speaking verse and the next minute he's coming in as the milkman. It's playful. Of course, the narrator is all-knowing. He is the one character on stage who knows the end of the story. He shares the audience's knowledge and he is commenting all the time. 'This is going to happen, don't get carried away. Having a great time are you? Don't forget that. . . .' But that was never written in a ponderous voice of doom kind of a way and the original stage directions said that it should be spoken idiomatically not in a BBC accent. It was all very simple. If we could do it on stage, we just did it. There's a moment where Eddie and Mickey go to see a porn movie and all we had was two actors and two chairs and a sound track and it creates cinema brilliantly in front of your eyes. Simplicity, simplicity, simplicity all the time. Just make the right stroke. Don't over dress it.

RM: Is it a Brechtian musical?

WR: It's Brechtian in the sense that he was another big influence on me. There was a debate at some point about is *Blood Brothers* a musical or is it a play with songs. It doesn't matter. It is what it is. Again, because of my knowledge of Brecht and the type of theatre that Joan Littlewood did, probably primarily *Oh! What a Lovely War*, and the work of people like McGrath and Chris Bond at the Everyman, it was just the done thing to include songs. You didn't have to call it a musical or a play with songs. When I'd written my first piece for the Everyman, *When the Reds*, an adaptation of an Alan Plater play, there had been a couple of songs in that but because I'd been functioning as a song writer for a long time, I just put lots more songs in. So it was completely natural for me to put songs in, the way Brecht did, but there is now all this theory around Brecht about what he is trying to achieve in terms of alienation technique. I wasn't doing that. I've always known that by using melody you can heighten and achieve a depth of emotion that without melody you would be hard pressed to achieve. Music is the most visceral of all the arts. It cuts through everything. Occasionally, you hear a speech that it is difficult to listen to without tears coming to your eyes, like Martin Luther King's 'I Have a Dream' for example, but the music of the voice is part of the reason that happens to you. There are not many speeches that will do that but any one of us can pass an open door, hear a snatch of music and be reduced to tears. I've always known that music has that power and I wanted to harness that because I wanted *Blood Brothers* to have big emotion. I wanted the audience to know we had been through something monumental together. Imagine if *Blood Brothers* ended with 'And do we blame superstition for what came to pass. . . .' You would want your money back. You have got to sing that grief, wail that grief. You have got to realize the anthemic, allow the elegiac to be given voice. 'Tell Me It's Not True' does nothing in terms of plot but it is totally crucial to the experience of engaging with *Blood Brothers*. The lives that I am depicting deserve music, something of the quasi-operatic. These are big, big events in the lives of these people and they are big lives therefore.

RM: Do you mind it being called a Greek tragedy?

WR: No although it's not a Greek tragedy because in strict Aristotelian terms there isn't a fall from grace. They are not elevated characters. Now in Arthur Miller's essay 'Tragedy and the Common Man', he argues that Willy Loman's fall is just as tragic and just as worthy as Hamlet's fall and I take that attitude, but I am just making the point that in the strict sense it is not a tragedy. But neither, because the word was sometimes applied pejoratively, is it a melodrama. It has elements, I think, of tragedy and of melodrama but it isn't strictly either of them.

Glen Walford (director)

Glen Walford (GW) is a freelance director who has directed many of Willy Russell's plays including more than ten versions of *Blood Brothers*, all abroad, several versions in Japan, two in Korea as well as productions in Germany and Siberia.

RM: What is it about the play that means it can connect to people, say, in Japan where you are going to direct your tenth production next year?

GW: One of the reasons the play resonates so well with an audience who doesn't know Liverpool are the themes which are epic, or we could say mythical, in their scope. It is operatic in its nature and it is Greek tragedy in its nature and it is funny too. All of these things help it to speak to people who don't necessarily know the details of where it is set. It deals, for example, with death which is symbolized through the guns and the kid's game and, of course, the deaths at the end. So we are taken into an immense realm of life and death. Then on another level there are themes which affect everyone on a more day to day level, like education. It looks at the differences in education between how a privileged child is educated and how poor kids are just ignored and how dependent you are on where you are placed in society in terms of how you grow up and what happens to you. So, focusing in on Sammy and Mickey, both of them have masses of imagination and if they were in an education system that respected that, instead of focusing only the rational, then they would own the world. So, it is also about how much an education system should value the power of the imagination over the rational and learning through imagination. The play is such a complex weaving of themes that there's almost nothing it isn't about.

RM: Is there anything you change when directing the show abroad?

GW: The key is never to try to do what separates cultures but look for what brings them together. I think it's unnecessary to change everything, even names of places, to suit the local culture. Just think how upset you would be if you went to see a play set in Japan and they had changed all the references because they thought you wouldn't understand or be able to connect to the themes in the play. People are perfectly happy with seeing Liverpool brought to life on stage because in their own imaginations they will equate Liverpool with whatever equates to them. Of course, they do have some images of Liverpool. They will know all about the Beatles more than anything and they will know all about Liverpool football team and they'll know that Liverpool has good comedians but I don't really think it is necessary that they do. It's like going to Narnia or somewhere. The Liverpool thing is a land that you open up for them on stage, so by the end of the play they will know something about Liverpool. It's not always necessary that you know all the details about the culture it is coming from because theatre is fundamentally about the power of imagination. If someone says to me, 'Hello, I am Hamlet', I'll buy it and think, well, invite me into your story. So, *Blood Brothers* is not just a Liverpool play. It is a global play about the human condition that belongs to everybody as Shakespeare does. He borrowed things from all over the world. He wanted to put a tiger in the Forest of Arden in *As You Like It* so he put one there without regard to the limiting parameters of boring fact. Willy doesn't rigidly lock himself into Liverpudlianism. He is Liverpool born and bred, it is in his blood and he loves the city but he certainly reaches way beyond that particular place. And however far away you are from Liverpool there are things in the play you can and will connect to. That is the vital thing.

RM: But there must be some things which an audience, say in Japan, finds harder to connect to?

GW: Of course there are differences. So, for example, in Japan, they don't have experience of class or they say they don't but they do because they have a tradition of the rich, noble families and samurais and all of that and it is all class. But they don't relate to it in the same way. Yet, they get the differences when they see the differences between Eddie and Mickey on stage. They see it coming alive in the costumes of the twins and the behaviour of Mrs Johnstone and of Mrs Lyons and of Eddie when he is at home with his dictionary and the very adult way Mr and Mrs Lyons try to respond to a boy whereas Mrs Johnstone is instinctive with the way she responds because she is a kid herself.

RM: So the characters then help an audience abroad connect to the play?

GW: Of course. If you are studying character in *Blood Brothers* which is an important way to look at it, you will see that they are the kinds of characters you can find all over the world. Take Sammy for example. The audience should like Sammy, which might sound strange considering his wild, anti-social behaviour, but if they don't respond lovingly to Sammy then Willy's point is lost because the kids follow Sammy and they don't follow Sammy because he is a bully – although he is. But if you look at Sammy, you will see there is much more to him than we might see on the surface. You'll see he is scared of women and that he is also utterly charming because he is funny as well, and imaginative.

RM: Isn't it true that all of the characters are more complicated and more multi-faceted than they first appear?

GW: The characters are very, very complex and how you portray them or think about them is important. So, with Mrs Lyons, when she's singing about imagining her child and holding him, there should be a real sense of a mother's love for her children. And also in the scene with Mrs Johnstone when she is saying the most heart wrenching things like when he was a child I used to look at him and think he knows that he is not really mine, he knows I have taken him from his real mother. In both those moments there is much more to Mrs Lyons than simply being the bad character.

RM: Is there something in the structure of the play that helps the audience connect?

GW: One of the things that helps the play feel so universal is the narrator who is such a non-specific character, and in my productions I have often looked for ways to enhance that role. So, as in the original production, the band is always on stage and fully visible. They play either side of the cut-outs of the roofs of the houses and you can see all of them. They are involved in the action. They throw balls down and they throw the babies down at the beginning. It adds to the theatricality of the performance but it also helps create more focus on the narrator's role. In the last production I did the narrator spent quite a bit of time on the roof with the band and she (it was a woman who played the role in that production) was much more highlighted by being with them. I have also brought an entire Greek chorus on in the production in Siberia to highlight emotions and the moments.

RM: You were in Liverpool in the 1980s, as artistic director of the Everyman Theatre, so you saw the first production of *Blood Brothers*. What was Liverpool like?

GW: To me it seemed very broken down when I went up there. It had a spirit of course because it has always had that. I had a love–hate relationship with the place because some days you were just depressed beyond belief about how run down everything was and how it was despised by the rest of the country, never given enough money, never given enough respect. The Everyman was so special and you just got on with the work that you wanted to do, you got on with weaving dreams no matter how decrepit it all was. And there was an incredible spirit there. There was no question about the humour and the courageous resilience. It was all there. It was a most important time in my whole life and I wouldn't have stayed there so long if it hadn't been.

I saw the very first production of *Blood Brothers* at the Liverpool Playhouse and thought it was wonderful. It zipped along at a cracking pace at the same time conveying the poignancy and depth in all the characters. Barbara Dickson as Mrs Johnstone pulled on the audience's heart-strings with her glorious voice and deeply felt love for her children. I knew then that I would like to direct it myself but didn't realize that I would still be directing many variations of it all these years later and in many parts of the globe.

RM: Why does Blood Brothers still connect to an audience today?

GW: It works, the same way Shakespeare still works because the story, the characters, the music, the humour, the tragedy resonates with the audience. I don't think you can pin this down to notions of 'relevance'. If it's good it is going to connect. There's a story about a kid who had seen *Blood Brothers* in

Japan and wrote to the chairman of Shochiku company who had put the play on and said he wanted to see *Blood Brothers* again and asked if they could revive it. The chairman actually wrote back to him and said yes we are going to do it in a couple of years and the child wrote back saying he was really pleased they were doing it again and sent a sketch he had done of two little boys standing together in a corner looking out into a world of nothing but with hope and love. This sketch went on the front of the next programme and it's my favourite *Blood Brothers* front. It's a picture of how you want Eddie and Mickey to be. You wish they could be together and that's what this little boy in Japan had seen when he watched the show which is a testament to the universality of the play.

Peter Treganna (actor)

Peter Treganna (PT) played Edward for a year in 1993/4 in the production that marked both the tenth anniversary of the original production in Liverpool and the fifth anniversary of Bill Kenwright's production in the West End.

RM: As an actor do you look at your character in a systematic way before you start rehearsing?

PT: You have to. I had about five days from the time I was cast until we started rehearsing. I had seen the show two or three years earlier, so I had an idea about the production but it was very vague, so the first thing was just reading the script again to familiarize myself with the story. Then I focused on the scenes I was in initially to see the character development. First, I identified what age he was in each scene and then read each scene through to myself, trying to think about what his character had done prior to walking on stage because what you are trying to do is build up and flesh out the character. The words are there but you need to find out who that character is. Obviously when he's a seven year old I looked at what his life would have been like up to that point. There are lots of clues in the script. The father's not been around when Mrs Lyons is 'pregnant' but there is a strong sense that he's not had too much to do with bringing up his son. I suppose I saw Eddie as a product of his parental upbringing.

RM: Are there some specific things you thought about in relation to Edward as a young boy that helped you understand the character?

PT: One of them was thinking about the kind of school he was at. Mickey's at the local state primary school. Eddie was in his cap and smart shorts and jumper and tie, so he is obviously being educated in a different kind of school. While it doesn't say it in the script, my thoughts were that because he came from a privileged background and was going to go to a boarding school, he was at preparatory school in Liverpool. Under those circumstances, you start to think of the people you know who had been to prep school. I'd been to a state school but I knew kids who had been to prep school and I thought about how my experiences of knowing them might help me understand Eddie. What you try and find is how somebody like that would react under certain circumstances.

Creating a character on stage, like discovering them through reading the script, is a process. The rehearsal period was short, so there was still development going on over the first months in performance where you were finding new things. It is a process in that a play is never complete without an audience and there are certain things you only discover when you are performing. So, for example, there are scripted laughs but there are also the laughs you get when you are before an audience who respond to things that happen, to your mannerisms and the inter-action between characters.

RM: What kind of mannerisms did Eddie have?

PT: I played him as being terribly proper. You wanted to play up the contrast between the rough kid Mickey who is super streetwise and Eddie who was prim and proper and had never been exposed to someone like Mickey before or met kids in gangs. I used to imagine him as playing chess and cricket with strict teachers and strict parents who perhaps were a little more distant emotionally and physically than Mickey's mother.

He has been very cossetted in his life, overly protected, dominated by his parents. He hasn't been given the opportunity to run free. So he is quite tight as a person. He has grown up in an environment where manners counted so he is very polite. All of that makes Eddie into someone who, in the first half of the show, is physically quite straight, not someone who is fluid. He's someone who stands to attention, almost like a little soldier. I was very aware that the early scenes took place in the early 60s, only fifteen years or so after the end of the war and at a time when National Service had only just finished.[4] In those days, kids from Eddie's background tended to have parents who were relatively stiff and they pushed that on to their kids. Kids didn't have flexibility, even in the way they communicated with adults. Eddie knew that he had to say please and thank you. He was freaked out and worried about the police when Mickey talked about doing anything naughty.

RM: But he quite likes that as well?

PT: I think his eyes are opened to a different way. With Mickey, he has the curtains drawn away from this whole other world that he's had no experience of but as he does experience it he gets a real buzz from it. I think this is why he sort of falls in love with Mickey in the way you fall in love with those people you meet in life who bring something remarkable into your life and change your perceptions.

---

[4] National Service came into existence after World War Two and meant that all men between the ages of 17 and 21 had to serve 18 months in the Armed Forces. It ended in 1960.

RM: So, as an actor you start with the script and thinking about what you can find out about the character?

PT: Yes. You identify what the script says in as much detail as possible about the character. You can pick that up from what he says, from where other people refer to him and also the way people react to him and that gives you the skeleton of the character.

RM: How does Eddie's character change as he grew up?

PT: When they meet again, it is about the gaucheness of adolescence. You've got Mickey who already has some kind of relationship with Linda and has developed in some ways and you've got Eddie who has no experience with girls at all. He sees this super cool guy who seems much more at ease on certain levels. There is still some of that imbalance you've seen between them at seven but I figured that by this time people who go to public school develop this innate confidence engendered by the public school system but that very often is more like a shell. Inside there is a whole raft of other things going on. For those scenes I thought about this guy I had met one summer who had been at Eton. Eddie hadn't been at Eton but he had been at a boarding school. He came across as just so inherently confident in some ways but if he encountered things that were out of his normal experience, he could be incredibly unconfident.

RM: Are they both a bit more similar at fourteen though? Mickey's also got a shell. He is a bit of a lad but doesn't know what to say to Linda.

PT: That's the interesting thing in the song, 'That Guy'. They want to be each other. And I think we also have to remember they are twins and the connection that can exist between twins is remarkable, even with those separated at birth. I think when they come together, on an unconscious level, they see the bits of them that are incomplete and the other one completes them.

RM: Does Eddie love Linda?

PT: He loves Linda and he loves Mickey. His love for Linda is that first boy/girl love. As far as we know he has no other experience with girls and he is blown away by Linda. He is really desperately keen to allow that love to develop but at the same time he can see the spark between Mickey and Linda and in the end, his affection for both of them means he sacrifices his own chances to help bring them together. There is also an element where he realizes that the reality of his existence means it could never happen. Probably deep down he was convinced that if he took Linda home, Mrs Lyons would not have been very happy. But overall, the intensity of his connection with Mickey is such that he would give Mickey the chance rather than himself. And, of course, Linda does love Mickey. They do end up having a light romance. When we were doing the show, inevitably I talked with the actor playing Linda [Emma Tate] about how far that romance goes. The script only says that something happens. We thought they probably had the odd kiss or two but nothing more. The script says they kick up leaves, which suggests something quite innocent.

When Mickey comes crashing into the Town Hall, Eddie is surprised and he's surprised that Mickey blames him for everything. From the audience's perspective, you have seen their lives and how they have been brought to where they are, but from Eddie's perspective he made none of the choices. He has just been put on this trajectory.

RM: So he's not to blame for what happens?

PT: I didn't think so. I felt sorry for Eddie in lots of ways because I think he didn't have freedom of choice in his life. Mickey did not have freedom of choice either but with Mickey there was a lot more freedom generally. Every time you see

Eddie, he is very tight and very tidy. He never really grows up. He's still the slightly gauche university student, lacking life experience. He's never had to worry about money and he's at that point in his life where he's not got to take responsibility for anything even after university. We're never told what job he does but the inference is that it is a management job and there's a sense that his father's got him the job and helped him become a councillor. One of the things I used to think is that if he had lived, Eddie might have moved to London and been part of the Big Bang in the City. He comes from that sort of background. It was still relatively rare to go to university in those days but in the end, he is very blasé in not really appreciating or understanding the reality of Mickey' life.

Things to do

In one of the interviews above, Glen Walford comments that *Blood Brothers* works 'the same way Shakespeare still works'. In groups, discuss any connections you can find between *Blood Brothers* and the Shakespeare play that you are studying. Think about aspects such as structure, character functions (e.g. contrasts), music, comedy and/or tragedy.

CHAPTER THREE

Writing About the Play

Although the specific questions asked change every year, you will always be asked to demonstrate certain skills and certain knowledge about the play. Examiners will expect you to show that you can:

- Develop an informed personal response, meaning you should have your own opinions about the play. These must be firmly located in evidence in the text (and the production if you have seen it) and in any further reading you have done.

- Illustrate your interpretation with appropriate evidence from the play. You need to be able to select the moments and quotations from the play that make your argument convincing.

- Analyse the key features of the play showing how the playwright has created meaning and effect through the use of dramatic devices such as language and structure and, in the case of *Blood Brothers*, music and song.

- Show an understanding of the relationship between the text and the time when it was written (its context).

- Write in an appropriately formal style using suitable vocabulary and terminology, keeping an eye on your spelling, punctuation and grammar.

Developing a personal response

As you study the play, it is important to give yourself time to develop your own opinion. You can do this in a number of ways. Most important is to read the text through carefully a number of times. It is useful to keep a notebook, to write down your thoughts and impressions as you are reading; by the time you have studied the play in detail you will have forgotten your first thoughts and these can be important to show how your ideas have changed and developed. It is also helpful to act out the play with some classmates. Even a few scenes will help you get a feel for how the language sounds and how different interpretations can be found in the same lines. It will also help you to think about the physical relationships between characters and how meaning can be found in where the characters are placed in a space, whether they look at each other as they speak or how close they might stand to each other.

Discussions in small groups or with the whole class can also help you develop your own ideas. Do make contributions as this will help you think about how you make your own argument and what evidence you might need to persuade somebody to agree with your point of view. Do also listen to what others say as this will help you think about other ways of understanding the play. In the end, there are very few points of view that are totally wrong as long as you can provide evidence from the play to back it up

Finding evidence in the text

Things to do

Look at the scene where the agreement is made between Mrs Johnstone and Mrs Lyons (pp. 35–40), and consider what you can discover about their characters. You should look not only at the dialogue (i.e. what is said) but also at the stage directions (including how things are said) and what happens (i.e. the character's actions).

The dialogue and stage directions give us some of the information. Mrs Lyons, for example, calls Mrs Johnstone, 'Mrs J' suggesting familiarity coupled with a lack of concern about who she really is. She starts by showing some kindness for the worried cleaner, asking her to sit down, but once the idea of getting a child of her own is planted, she takes control, issuing commands, to get what she wants. She interrupts Mrs Johnstone, not allowing her a chance to refuse and thinking quickly of a series of reasons as to why it is a good idea. The speed with which she comes up with arguments suggests she is used to getting her own way and not above twisting what has been said to her to get what she wants. Her use of language, which is full of imperatives, such as 'give one of them to me' and 'quickly, quickly, tell me', establishes her control over Mrs Johnstone and makes it harder for Mrs Johnstone to say no (36). Yet, she is also uncertain. As she runs out of reasons, she simply says, 'Please, Mrs Johnstone. Please.' (36). Whilst she cannot then articulate her desperation in words, she can sing about her real feelings and her loneliness although as soon as she has revealed this she *gives a half smile and a shrug, perhaps slightly embarrassed at what she has revealed'* (37). Once Mrs Johnstone has agreed, she takes control again, telling her that 'from now on I do the shopping' (39). There is still a suggestion of her reliance on Mrs Johnstone when she has to ask for her advice in placing the cushion so she looks pregnant. This establishes a character who is complex, controlling and manipulative but also vulnerable and unhappy.

Mrs Johnstone is at a loss throughout much of the scene. She does not know what to do about the fact she is having twins, simply repeating the same idea in different ways from saying 'I had it all worked out' to 'we were just getting straight' (35). She loves her children but she is shown to be in a situation she cannot resolve herself. She is amused by Mrs Lyons suggestion, treating it as if it is *'almost a joke'* suggesting she does not have a firm grasp on reality (36). Looking around the house and seeing what life could be like for her child suggests an imaginative mind at work and her response to Mrs Lyons, when she opens up and tells her what she really feels, suggests a character who is sympathetic to others.

Actions also reveal important things about the characters. Mrs Lyons has two moments where her actions make us see something about her. Firstly, without even waiting for Mrs Johnstone to agree, she grabs a cushion and arranges it beneath her dress to suggest she is pregnant, implying little sympathy for Mrs Johnstone and a confidence that she will agree. Yet, at the moment Mrs Johnstone agrees she *'goes across and kisses her, hugs her'* showing how much this means to her (38). The most important action for Mrs Johnstone is a nod, when she assents to the plan. She cannot articulate the words, which could suggest that she is reluctant and has no choice, but the nod is preceded by a pause which suggests she is agreeing after thinking about it and having listened to what Mrs Lyons has said (or sung), even if she cannot quite bring herself to say the words. Maybe her reluctance to speak might suggest to you that she cannot admit to herself that this is happening, that she is not facing up to reality.

Quoting from the play

When you use quotations you will need to be clear about where they come from in the play, who is speaking and, at times, for clarity, who they are speaking to. Given the lack of scene numbers in *Blood Brothers*, it is easiest to locate quotations through describing the particular moment. For example, 'In the scene where the twins first meet, Edward says . . .' or 'when the twins come out of the cinema they are chanting . . .' Do not forget that it is **you** who are quoting the play and not the characters; they are saying or shouting or exclaiming or singing – or whatever tone you envisage they are using at this point.

Make sure that the quotation you use makes the point you want to make and then make that point explicit, providing an explanation for the reader, in what you say next. For example, you might say: 'By saying this, Mrs Johnstone shows she is not very responsible.' You do not need to make your own thought process clear, so you do not need to say things like 'I have chosen this quote to show that . . .' as the quotation and your explanation make this clear to the reader.

The best way to learn quotes is by acting out the play and learning the lines gradually as an actor would. In the examination you will be expected to quote briefly from memory, so it is useful to identify some short key quotations that illustrate themes or characters. Look for quotations that will explain something rather than just tell the story. So, for example, in the scene where Linda tries to persuade Mickey to come off the tablets, rather than picking Mickey saying he 'can't do without them', the more interesting quotation might be Mickey keeps taking the tablets so he 'can be invisible' because it says more about his state of mind (122–3). It is also useful to try and embed your quotations in the sentence you are writing as it makes the essay more fluent, so your argument is easier to follow. For example, 'When the twins meet up again at Christmas, Mickey tells Edward he wishes he could still believe in "all that blood brother stuff" but he cannot "because while no one was looking I grew up". It was all just "kids" stuff.' (115).

Analysing the playwright's techniques

One of the things you will be asked to consider is *how* the playwright creates meaning and effect. This means considering not just *what* they communicate to the audience but also *how* this is communicated – how they use dramatic techniques such as set, costume, lighting, language, music and structure. Two examples are considered below but there is more on this in the section on dramatic structure.

Music

When the twins meet up again, Russell uses the song 'That Guy' to allow the twins to voice their own thoughts without the other one hearing, in a device that is called a soliloquy. The song also allows for the differences and the similarities between the twins to be expressed. Although they are, on the face of it, singing individually about what is wrong with them, from acne to bad breath, and they are physically separate to each other, eyeing each other up, the song has them singing together. Because it is a sung, rather than spoken, the audience can also hear them singing the same tune and singing in harmony in a way that suggests that despite their physical separation they are connected.

Structure

The play has a cyclical structure, i.e. it starts at the same point that it ends. It uses the same lines from the narrator and Mrs Johnstone repeats 'Tell me it's not true.' Both of these dramatic techniques create a sense of inevitability and fate. Russell also uses dramatic irony where the characters know less than the audience (they are 'in' on the secret). This adds to the tension as they wait for the characters to discover the truth. The action also flows seamlessly with no scene breaks, helping to create a sense of moving towards the inescapable conclusion. Russell's use of an episodic structure, where the play jumps through time, also helps the audience to compare the twins at various stages of their lives as they move along their different paths. This is helped by the use of parallel scenes. In the section on schools, there are two adjoining scenes that allow for comparison between the twins' experience and in the section where, as Mickey agrees to go on the job with Sammy, which is intercut with Edward telling Linda that he has always loved her, their lives become even more intertwined.

Moving from description to analysis

For most people, our first response when we are asked about something we have read is to tell the story, to describe what happens in it. This is different to analysing or evaluating which is what you are being asked to do in essays and examinations. For example, it would be descriptive to say that Mrs Johnstone stands by herself on stage as the children complain from off-stage that the baby is crying or that all the other kids laugh at them for having free school meals. Description is a matter of fact. It is objective. You are saying what you can see or hear or what you have read. If you were to analyse this moment, you would start to offer suggestions about what it might mean or signify and you might start to think about how it shows Mrs Johnstone as being alone (we know her husband has left her) – with the burden of having to deal with her large family by herself with very little money. If you were to evaluate this scene, you would start to form a critical judgement of it and to think about how it might show something about her character. Why does she stay outside the house and not go in to comfort her children who say they are starving and cannot sleep? Why is her first response to their distress to tell them not to swear? Is there something in this moment that suggests a 'bad' mother? Or a mother who cannot cope? She goes on to spin stories about food to come, a fantasy fairy tale bedtime story to pacify them, so does this say something different about her? All these questions suggest something about the process of evaluation; it is much more subjective than description and therefore moments can be open to a variety of interpretations. However, whatever your answers to the questions, you need to be able to provide evidence to support what you think.

Things to do

Starting with the following descriptions use them to develop analysis and evaluation of the moments.

● The first time Mickey appears, aged 'seven', he is knocking incessantly at his front door and carrying a toy gun.

● As the twins go off to the cinema, Mrs Johnstone is left alone lilting the 'We Go Dancing' line.

● When Edward leaves to go to the country, he gives Mickey his toy gun.

From analysis to argument

We tend to think that an argument is a disagreement but an academic argument is different to falling out with a friend. It is a set of reasons that are offered to support a proposal or an idea; you might want to think about it as expressing a point of view which is backed up by evidence. It should be more ordered and more rational than an argument with someone you know (which can get very heated and emotional) and you should try and present both sides of an argument, for and against a particular point of view. Of course, in your conclusion you can come down heavily on one side or the other.

The best way to create a coherent argument is to take your time planning your work and you need to think about the points you want to make, the evidence to back these up and the order in which it will be most persuasive to offer these. In an examination, the temptation is to dive in and write as much as possible as quickly as possible, but taking some time to plan your argument will ensure you write a better answer. You are less likely to forget something important, more likely to organize your ideas clearly and more likely to understand what the question is asking you to do. Make sure you also leave yourself enough time at the end to read through what you have written to ensure your argument is made clearly.

Things to do

In the play find three pieces of evidence to back up the following claims:

- *Blood Brothers* suggests that nature is stronger than nurture.

- Mrs Johnstone is to blame for the death of the twins.

- The Lyons family is used to present the middle class in a negative light.

Now find three pieces of evidence that offer a different point of view. In class, present your findings as a debate, for and against each statement. At the end, you might want to decide which argument was more persuasive.

Connecting the text to the context

All works of art can be seen as a product of the times and place they were written in. You cannot fully understand *Blood Brothers*, if you ignore the impact of Margaret Thatcher and particularly her impact on cities like Liverpool. Whilst the play is a dramatic fiction and not a history book, the world Russell was living in is reflected in the play, particularly because *Blood Brothers* is a play that deals with social issues like class and life chances. The most obvious way it connects is in the section dealing with unemployment, but this is not the only way and for an audience watching the play in Liverpool Playhouse in 1983 there would have been a web of connections to be made to the world they found themselves in. This is true reading the play today. Context can relate to the time you read or see the play in as well, a connection made by a reviewer in 2013 who noted that with all its talk of guns, job losses and human misery 'you could easily think that *Blood Brothers* was set in Cameron's Britain' (Wright, 2013).

Ideally, when you write about context, you should refer to it in the body of your writing rather than in a separate paragraph. So, if you are writing about education and class, you might want to discuss what you have learned about secondary modern schools. You are trying to show how the context is integrally linked to the play, so it should be discussed in this way and not as something that is an after-thought or bolted on. It is central to understanding the text.

Things to do

Discuss the ways in which you can see the ideas of *Blood Brothers* reflected in the world you find yourselves. You may want to consider issues such as opportunities in education, attitudes to single parents and childhood, unemployment and poverty, belief in superstitions (or urban myths) or the attitude of the police to people from different classes.

Writing with appropriate formality

In *Blood Brothers,* there is plenty of swearing and slang and colloquialisms but in writing an essay, you need to adopt a much more formal tone. Of course, you will want to capture the flavour of the play (and language is important in *Blood Brothers*) but this can be done through quotations or by putting quotation marks around a word that is used in the text. So for example, Edward giggles with glee when Mickey whispers 'the F word' to him or Mickey's 'Mam' is very optimistic. Some other key things to remember when you are writing include:

- You should use the present tense when you are writing about the play (try to think about it as if it is a living thing happening in front of your eyes). For example, 'Edward goes away to university' not 'Edward went away to university'. There are times when you may need to use the past tense; for example, referring to the play's context or the first production. So, 'By 1978, Liverpool had the highest unemployment rate in the country' or 'The gauze for the first production of the play carried an image of Marilyn Monroe.'

- Write in complete sentences and use paragraphs. Start a paragraph for each new idea and ensure that these all take your argument forward.

- You are asked to develop a personal response to the play but when you are writing it is not always helpful to write in the first person (i.e. I think that . . .). More objective writing helps to give your writing more force and rigour adding a greater authority to your argument and focuses more on the play than on your subjective (personal) thinking. Useful phrases to help you do this might include:

  The study of *Blood Brothers* reveals . . .

  In this essay, it will be argued that Mrs Johnstone's belief in superstition causes the death of the twins (instead of 'In this essay, I will discuss . . .')

  This essay considers . . .

  It can be imagined/argued that . . .

- Your own voice will still be apparent from *what* you argue and the points that you make. There are times when using 'I' can be helpful. You might, for example, want to refer to your own response to a moment in the production you have seen or to your initial response to reading the text. For these moments of personal experience, the use of 'I' is useful and pertinent.

Tell Me It's Not True . . . a final word

When you are writing about the play, don't forget that it is a play and not real life. Aristotle in the *Poetics* uses the term mimesis (like mime or mimic) or imitation to explain what is distinctive about our experience of art. Art or drama presents us with a version of reality but at one remove from it. We know when we are in the theatre that we are watching not Mrs Johnstone but an actor playing Mrs Johnstone (they stand on stage and bow to us at the end, including the twins who have just 'died') and the character is a construct created by the writer. After all, when Mickey kills Edward we do not rush out to call the police (who are there already!) but if we saw someone shot on the street we would.

And do not forget that it is a play and not a novel. This means that when you are writing about it, you need to be able to talk about both what you have read on the page but also what happens (or what might happen) on the stage because the play is written to be performed. It is about both words and actions. For example, if you are writing about superstition, do not forget that quite often when things happen to the characters, the narrator is on stage and visible to the audience as a reminder. Or if you are writing about dancing, there is also dancing in the show that is not necessarily evident in the script. Think about the stagecraft of the writer and about the impact of the play on the audience who are *watching*. If you have been lucky enough to see the play, remember what it felt like and what you saw as well as what you heard.

Above everything else, do not forget to enjoy studying and thinking about the play! Studying a play can sometimes be frustrating, so it is worthwhile stopping occasionally and trying to recapture your thoughts on first reading or seeing the play. *Blood Brothers* is a comedy as well as a tragedy, so there should be plenty of laughs as well as tears.

BIBLIOGRAPHY

Aristotle translated by Kenneth McLeish (1998) *Poetics*, London: Nick Hern Books.

Beryl Bainbridge (2006) *Front Row: Evenings at the Theatre: Pieces from The Oldie*, London: Continuum.

Michael Billington (1983) Review of *Blood Brothers*, *Guardian*, 12 April.

Michael Billington (2007) *State of the Nation: British Theatre Since 1945*, London: Faber and Faber.

Berthold Brecht (edited and translated by John Willett, 1986) *Brecht on Theatre: The Development of an Aesthetic*, London: Eyre Methuen.

Georgina Brown (1998) Review of *Blood Brothers* at Phoenix Theatre, *Mail on Sunday*, 2 August.

John Burgess (2005) *The Faber Pocket Guide to Greek and Roman Drama*, New York: Faber and Faber.

Jim Cartwright (1996) *Plays: 1*, London: Methuen.

John Gill (1992) *Willy Russell and His Plays*, Birkenhead: Countrywise.

Steve Grant (1983) Review of *Blood Brothers* at Lyric Theatre, *Plays and Players*, April.

John Gross (1998) Review of *Blood Brothers* at Phoenix Theatre, *Daily Telegraph*, 2 August.

Les Harding (2012) *They Knew Marilyn Monroe*, New York: McFarland.

Brian Logan (1998) Review of *Blood Brothers* at Phoenix Theatre, *Observer*, 2 August.

Andrew Marr (2008) *A History of Modern Britain*, London: Pan Macmillan.

Arthur Miller (1994) 'Tragedy and the Common Man' in *The Theater Essays of Arthur Miller*, London: Methuen.

Jane Milling (2012) *Modern British Playwriting: The 1980s*, London: Methuen.

Sheridan Morley (1998) Review of *Blood Brothers* at Phoenix Theatre, *Spectator*, 8 August.

Jim Mulligan (2005) Interview with Willy Russell, *The Collected Interviews of Jim Mulligan* http://www.jimmulligan.co.uk/interview/willy-russell-blood-brothers

John Murden (2006) 'City of Change and Challenge: Liverpool Since 1945' in John Belchem (ed.) *Liverpool 800: Culture, Character and History*, Liverpool: Liverpool University Press.

Benedict Nightingale (1998) Review of *Blood Brothers* at Phoenix Theatre, *The Times*, 30 July.

Paul du Noyer (2004) *Liverpool Wondrous Place: Music from the Cavern to the Coral*, London: Virgin.

Jasper Rees (2010) 'Willy Russell Interview', *Daily Telegraph*, 24 March.

David Roper (1983) 'Alive to the Sound of Music', *Daily Express*, 14 April.

Willy Russell (1996) *Plays: 1*, London: Methuen.

Peter Taylor (1998) 'Scouse Folk Opera', *The Independent*, 30 July.

Jack Tinker (1988) Review of *Blood Brothers* at The Albery, *Daily Mail*, 29 July.

Tim Walker (2009) 'A Boost for Blood Brothers', *Sunday Telegraph*, 20 November.

Irving Wardle (1983) 'Twins Caught in a Fatal Trap', *The Times*, 12 January.

Jade Wright (2013) Review of *Blood Brothers* at Liverpool Empire, *Liverpool Echo*, 29 October.

INDEX

www.ingramcontent.com/pod-product-compliance
Ingram Content Group UK Ltd.
Pitfield, Milton Keynes, MK11 3LW, UK
UKHW020712280225
455688UK00012B/351